BRONWYN FOX

POWER OVER PANIC

FREEDOM FROM PANIC/ANXIETY RELATED DISORDERS

Shakti River Press
A Divison of
Transpersonal Learning & Counseling Services

Shakti River Press
A Division of Transpersonal Learning and Counseling Services
P.O. Box 477
Saratoga CA 95071-0477
Copyright © U.S. Edition 1999
Shakti River Press
Copyright © Australian Edition 1996
Addison Wesley Longman Australia Pty. Ltd.
Designed by Jan Schmoeger/Designpoint/Australia
Printed by Banta Book Group
ISBN 09627327-1-0.
Library reference
616.85223
Fox, Bronwyn

Bronwyn Fox may be reached at
Panic Anxiety Education and Management Service
P.O. Box 258
Fullarton, So. Australia 5063
E-mail: fox@camtech.net.au/index html
Web: http//www.paems.com.au

Contents

Acknowledgements

The case histories in this book are true, although the names have been changed to ensure privacy to the individuals concerned. I express my appreciation and thanks to the many people who, like myself, have had or now have panic disorder/agoraphobia, for sharing their histories with me. Not only have you increased my own understanding of the disorder, you have also taught me much about myself.

My thanks also to Christopher Edwards, Clinical Psychologist, Associate Professor Julian Hafner, Professor Larry Evans and the Board of the Anxiety Disorders Foundation of Australia Inc. for their commitment and dedication to ensuring that recognition and treatment of anxiety disorders are available to everyone who needs them.

Lastly, specific thanks to Jasmin Arthur-Jones, Anthony Byrne, former CEO of the Anxiety Disorders Foundation of Australia Inc., Carol Barker, Joy Little and the Committee of PADA Inc. for their help, friendship, support and encouragement.

To Dr Eli Rafalowicz

'We paced along the lonely plain, as one who returns to his lost road, and till he reaches it, seems to go in vain.'

Danté, 'Purgatorio' in the *Divine Comedy*

Preface to the U.S. Edition

This small but mighty book offers the keys to freedom for those who are tired of struggling alone with anxiety, who seek to discover the secret of their own empowerment, and who hope to break loose from the limitations of anxiety and panic disorders. It also introduces the use of meditation, both "mantra" and mindfulness models, as a tool for recovery. It teaches you how to use these time-tested methods that promote peace and balance and bring them into every activity of your life.

A famous Australian actor, Garry McDonald, found this process so healing in his own life (after twenty years of suffering with anxiety) that he offered to write a foreword, published first in the Australian edition, which made the best-seller list in Australia in 1998.

The author, Bronwyn Fox, is a remarkable woman who is dedicated to transforming clinical understanding of anxiety and panic disorder, which is a major international health issue shared by millions of ordinary people. Following a life-threatening illness, Bronwyn was debilitated by crippling surges of energy and heat, heart palpitations, depersonalization (a feeling of being detached from the body), derealization (a feeling you and/or your surroundings are not real) and overwhelming terror for several years. As she searched for the secrets of returning to normal health, she discovered a remarkable combination of simple practices and therapies that led her to major life changes and ultimately empowered her to become a writer and international speaker and workshop facilitator. She developed a program for research and for helping people into recovery. She became a major innovator and made significant contributions to this field of mental health in Australia.

Bronwyn's message, which has brought hope and health to many thousands of people in Australia, is very clear. You have the ability to change how you think, to release how you feel, to quiet your mind and to do whatever you truly wish to do with your life. The fear is real. The energy is real. The panic attack is real. You are not crazy. And you can overcome the problems. You just need the tools to be with your body in a new way.

Her simple, five-step process can be learned and applied by anyone and offers an entirely new perspective to most of those who follow it. In an extensive study in Australia, 97% of those who participated in a survey three months after completing her workshop reported they had been helped by the program, and also reported a significant reduction across all symptom groups.

As a counselor I have seen the devastating pain for individuals caught in the downward spiral of fear of their own body. As a transpersonal therapist and educator I have come to recognize that the vital energy and consciousness in each of us can become subject to spontaneous radical and transformative change. I believe that most of us can move through our limitations and fears if we just have good guidance suggesting useful perspectives and practices.

As a publisher of books dedicated to helping people understand themselves and live their lives more fully, I feel that it is a great privilege to offer this book in the United States. I believe it offers not only the steps for healing but a bridge into a stronger and healthier sense of self. Bronwyn is a living testimony to her work. If you recognize your problems in her book, you need to recognize your potential in her own transformed life. These changes require some courage and self-discipline, releasing some of the tight control of your life in order to really be yourself. If you can set an intention, you can do it.

A crisis in our lives is a profound message from the deep unconscious forcing us to become more introspective and to discover more of our true capacity and potential. Sometimes these are energies of the psyche--encouraging us to become more individuated, more full as human beings. Sometimes they are energies of the spirit--showing us other dimensions of consciousness--encouraging us to recognize our selves as spiritual beings.

Whether your work is at the psychological or spiritual level --- and for me the line between the two is transparent -- recovery from your anxiety and your panic attacks includes recovery of parts of yourself. The secret of true growth is the transmutation of fear and the release of contraction around change. Bronwyn's five steps are the simple alchemical methods for regaining the forward momentum in your life.

We encourage you to work with a therapist trained in cognitive-behavioral work or to find group therapy focused on recovery as an adjunct to this book. Find someone you can trust and relate to and share this book with him/her, developing an ally for your healing. It may be you have not found just the right support as you have struggled to understand this disorder--but know now that you are not alone, millions of others share this problem, and you are not mentally ill. You need understanding, calming, retraining and acceptance--and you can find your way back to health. Find a therapist who can share this vision with you!

It is with great pleasure that Shakti River Press brings this practical and powerful message to the millions in the United States and Canada that have not yet met Bronwyn Fox. A list of referral sources of specialists for anxiety and panic disorders is included as an appendix. Don't wait another day.

Bonnie Greenwell, Ph.D.
Publisher: Shakti River Press
Director: Transpersonal Learning & Counseling Services

Foreword

by Garry McDonald

This is a truly wonderful book. I mean, just look at it! It contains an easily manageable five-step plan to recovery, it's just over one hundred pages long and you can read it in under an hour.

Most of the other books on anxiety disorders I've come across are at least three times as long, contain too many varying techniques, or even worse, narrowly focus on one, and are full of erudite medical, psychiatric and/or psychological references. Attempting to read them was enough to *give* me a panic attack.

When I first read this book I felt such a tremendous sense of relief and joy. I wasn't mad, I wasn't imagining it, I was definitely not a drama queen, I wasn't alone and *my disorder* was treatable without medication.

No one in the medical profession—neither my GP, my psychiatrist nor psychologist—had actually explained to me what was wrong with me. It was all there in this book.

The case histories show you what a large cross-section of the public have this disorder, from the young to the elderly, students to very successful career people; and the text shows how you can recover and take charge of your life once more.

I had been suffering from an anxiety disorder for over twenty years. I'd been put on various tranquilizers and sleeping pills. The first psychologist I was referred to told me all I needed to do was surround myself with co-workers I trusted; increase my power base. Great advice—co-dependency!

The next therapist I had tried a bit of everything, self-esteem work, a bit of positive thinking, even waving a finger in front of my eyes while I alternatively thought negative and positive thoughts, and then finally the *coup de grace*, I was advised to try wearing a rubber band around my wrist. Whenever I felt an approaching panic attack I was to pull the rubber band taught and release it so it would sting my inside wrist. The ensuing pain would divert my attention from the panic attack.

I am very pleased to say none of these techniques appear in this book. Oh, by the way, if anyone is interested I still have a box of as-new number twelve rubber bands I would be willing to part with for a greatly reduced amount—let's see, the therapist charged me $80.00 for the session—let's say $40.00. Generous Huh?

I've been very annoyed at the ignorance of the medical profession when it comes to anxiety disorders and their treatment. Mind you, it wasn't so long ago that people with anxiety disorders were considered the 'worried well' by both governments and some health professionals—an extraordinarily ignorant phrase considering 12% of the population experience an anxiety disorder and the suicide attempt rate for people with anxiety disorders is higher than any other mental health problem.

Now I'm pleased to say that with appropriate therapy in the form of cognitive behavioral techniques, relaxation, various forms of exposure and most importantly, cognitive restructuring, people can recover. I can testify to this fact. I *recovered* within eight weeks of starting this treatment.

Bronwyn Fox knows what she is talking about. She had an anxiety disorder. Not only has she written this marvellous book, but she was instrumental in setting up the largest self-help organization in Australia, the Panic Anxiety Disorder Association Inc, PADA, and more recently helped in the formation of the Anxiety Disorders Foundation of Australia. She conducts programs and workshops throughout Australia where she teaches self-management techniques and PADA received a silver award from the Australian and New Zealand Mental Health Achievement Awards for her programs and workshops.

This is a great book that I heartily recommend to people with anxiety disorders, their loved ones and those in the caring professions.

GARRY MCDONALD

Part 1

Anxiety disorders and their effects

Chapter 1

Anxiety disorders

Panic disorder; generalized anxiety disorder; post traumatic stress disorder; obsessive compulsive disorder; and social phobia are classified as anxiety disorders. Anxiety disorders affect 12.6% per cent of the population over a twelve-month period (Andrews 1994). Research suggests anxiety disorders represent the largest mental health problem in the general population (APA 1980). Using the current Australian population figure of 18 million (ABS 1995), this means that 2.2 million people are affected by these disorders. The age of onset of the disorders is usually between the late teens and the mid thirties, although they have begun in childhood and as late as seventy.

Central to the anxiety disorders are the experience of panic attacks. Until the identification in 1994 of three separate and distinct types of panic attacks (APA 1994), all panic attacks were considered one and the same. The introduction of these three categories is a major step forward in the understanding of the subjective experience of these attacks.

Panic attacks

'Uncued'—spontaneous panic attacks

The experience of an uncued attack is the central feature of panic disorder. An uncued panic attack is an attack that occurs spontaneously, irrespective of what the person may be doing at the time. It is not triggered by situations and places. People who experience this type of attack may also experience them at night while asleep.

'Cued' panic attacks

Unlike the experience of a spontaneous attack, the cued attack does relate to and is triggered by specific situations or places. The cued attack is one of the components of post traumatic stress disorder, obsessive compulsive disorder and social phobia. It is unusual for people with panic disorder to experience this type of attack.

'Situationally predisposed panic attacks'

Some people may be predisposed to having panic attacks in some situations and/or places. The attack is not necessarily triggered by the particular situation and/or place and may happen on some occasions and not on others. People with spontaneous panic attacks may go on to develop this type of attack.

CASE HISTORIES

Carolyn

It had been a long and difficult week. Carolyn was glad she now had some time to herself. She curled up on the lounge with a book she had been wanting to read. As she relaxed she felt the tension ease from her body and she felt herself drifting into sleep. Without warning, she felt a wave of incredible energy surge through her body. As it moved through her, her heart rate doubled, she had difficulty breathing, she felt lightheaded and dizzy, a wave of nausea swept over her and she began to perspire. She jumped up and ran outside to her husband. 'Help me, something is happening to me, I don't know what but something is very wrong.'

Alex

Alex disliked staff meetings and social get togethers and did what he could to avoid them. He felt more comfortable just doing his job and avoiding any personal interaction with other staff. Now the new owners of the business had arranged a dinner for all staff and their partners and, like it or not, Alex had to go. He had been feeling uncomfortable all day and he knew his anxiety levels were very high. As he and his wife sat down at their table the people next to them began to make conversation. His heart began to race, his breathing became short and shallow, he began to perspire heavily and his hands trembled violently. As he tried to control it, he thought to himself, I shouldn't have come. This always happens every time I am in this situation.

Jessica

Jessica turned on the ignition of her car. She was feeling very anxious. Is it going to happen today? As she pulled out of her driveway she tried to rationalize with herself for the hundredth time. She wasn't frightened of driving, in fact she used to enjoy driving before she began to have spontaneous panic attacks. But there was one set of traffic lights where she would sometimes have an attack. There was no pattern to it. Sometimes it happened, sometimes it didn't. Sometimes she would have an attack after she had driven through the traffic lights; on other days there were no attacks at all. Someone had told her she was frightened of that particular intersection, but she thought that was ridiculous. She was frightened of the attacks and their unpredictable nature, it had nothing to do with the intersection.

Panic disorder

Central to panic disorder is the experience of spontaneous panic attacks. The attacks can be a result of a major life stress or a build-up of stress. People may have an attack months after an extremely stressful episode and never have another one. Other people may have intermittent attacks throughout their life, not necessarily at predictable times. A number of people have reported their panic attacks began while using marijuana.

Panic disorder is diagnosed after a person has experienced 'at least two' spontaneous panic attacks followed by one month of 'persistent concern' of having another one. Although it is not unusual for people who develop panic disorder to have two or more attacks a day and to experience pervasive anxiety in anticipation of having another one (APA 1994). Many people feel as if they are having a heart attack or they may die or go insane or lose control in some way.

Generalized anxiety disorder

Generalized anxiety disorder is diagnosed when a person experiences 'anxiety and worry for at least six months over particular real life events' such as marital or financial problems (APA 1994).

Post traumatic stress disorder

People suffering from post traumatic stress disorder can include Vietnam veterans, fire victims and victims of violent crime, sexual and/or physical abuse. People may experience flashbacks in which they believe they are actually living through the traumatic event again, or may have nightmares in which they relive the experience. They may also experience a cued attack when specific situations are reminiscent or similar to the traumatic event.

Panic disorder can be secondary to post traumatic stress disorder. On occasions people will seek treatment for their panic disorder but will be too frightened or ashamed to speak of the traumatic event which precipitated it. This is especially so in matters relating to childhood abuse. One English study showed 63.6% of young women with panic disorder who were interviewed for the study, came from 'difficult childhood backgrounds', which included 'parental indifference, sexual and physical abuse' (Brown et al 1993).

Obsessive compulsive disorder

Obsessive compulsive disorder means being obsessed by 'persistent ideas, thoughts, impulses, or images that cause marked anxiety or distress' (APA 1994). Unlike generalized anxiety disorder which is based upon 'real life' concerns, the obsessive thoughts can be a fear of contamination by germs, or a fear that the person might harm other people, or act in a socially unacceptable way. The person may experience a cued attack when confronted with their particular fear, such as a fear of contamination by germs.

In an attempt to reduce the anxiety or to ease the fears, people often develop compulsive rituals which may take up the entire day. People may wash their hands or brush their teeth until their hands or mouth bleed. Others may have to have everything arranged in a particular way, or the person may have to re-do certain jobs a number of times. They may feel the need to repeat a name or a phrase constantly. Others may continually check to see if they have locked their house or car, or if they have turned off their domestic appliances. Some people begin to hoard unwanted or useless items. These compulsions can be so severe that the person becomes totally restricted by them and is unable to lead a normal life.

Social phobia

Social phobia can also be an extremely restrictive disorder. People fear being watched by other people. They become frightened in case they embarrass themselves. They may fear public speaking, eating in front of other people, social occasions or talking to people. Some people are frightened to walk down the street or go into a shop in case people look at them. People can suffer extreme anxiety in these situations, and it is not unusual for them to experience 'cued' panic attacks.

Combinations

Although each disorder has its own primary manifestation, symptoms of other disorders can be experienced in conjunction with the principal disorder. A diagnosis is made by the primary presenting symptoms. Treatment will be directed to the primary disorder, along with associated treatment/s towards the overlap of the others.

This book is about what I have discovered about myself and other people who suffer from a panic-related anxiety disorder. It draws on my own and other people's experiences of the disorder. It is difficult to distinguish between the examples. The many people I have spoken to will recognize themselves, but so too will the many millions of other people who have the disorder.

Chapter 2

Anxiety vs Anxiety Disorders

The differences between them

Part of the overall problem in understanding the severity of the disorders lies in the word 'anxiety'. Everyone has been anxious at one time or another, and it is through our own experience of anxiety that we judge those who experience anxiety disorders.

Our own anxiety may not have affected us to any great extent. If it did we were able to do something about it, or it passed of its own accord and was no longer a problem. We have extreme difficulty in accepting that a person with an anxiety disorder experiences anything different from our own anxiety. So it is quite natural for us to say or think 'pull yourself together', or to ignore that there really is a problem.

There is a marked difference between the 'normal' experience of anxiety and that of an anxiety disorder. People cannot 'pull themselves together', because they do not know what is wrong with them. They do not recognize the symptoms as anxiety. If it was purely the experience of anxiety, people would recognize it and they would be able to address the problem. It is this difference which is highlighted by the fact that even now, some health professionals are still unable to recognize, let alone, diagnose or treat these disorders.

> The symptoms of anxiety can be quite varied, with any number of symptoms being experienced at the same time. The most common ones are a rapid or pounding heartbeat,

9

'missed' heartbeats, chest pain, an inability to take a deep
breath, a feeling that breathing will stop altogether, choking
sensation, dizziness, giddiness, feeling faint, nausea, pins
and needles, diarrhea, trembling hands and/or legs, dry
mouth, sweating, fatigue, loss of concentration, loss of
libido. Dissociative symptoms can include depersonalization
(feeling detached from the body), derealization (as if
everything about us is unreal), visual disturbance such as
intolerance to light, stationary objects appearing to move,
tunnel vision and/or audio disturbance, where every-day
noise seems louder than normal.

For many people with an anxiety disorder the symptoms are
their constant companion. Not just for a few minutes or hours at
a time, but ongoing sometimes for months or years. To confuse
the issue further, people can experience different symptoms and
sensations in their anxiety and panic attacks (Arthur-Jones 1994).

Secondary conditions

It is the lack of diagnosis and the lack of adequate treatment
services which is the driving force behind the development of the
secondary conditions of these disorders. Although the symptoms
of panic disorder were first noted in the 1800s (Boyd et al. 1991),
panic disorder was only classified as a separate anxiety disorder
by the American Psychiatric Association in February 1980 (APA
1980). As a consequence there was little understanding of it, not
only by the people who suffer from it, but by the health professions
generally. Many people have developed secondary conditions
such as agoraphobia, major reactive depression, and drug and/or
alcohol abuse.

The development of major depression can lead to suicide.
According to one American study, 26.5 per cent of people who
experience panic disorder will attempt suicide. People who have
not been diagnosed as suffering from panic disorder, but who
nevertheless experience panic attacks, are seven times more
likely than the general population to attempt suicide (Malison et
al. 1990). Other studies confirm that 10–40 per cent of people
with an alcohol dependence had an anxiety-related disorder
before their dependence developed (Cox et al. 1990).

The recognition of the sometimes severe disabilities associated
with anxiety disorders has seen the inclusion of the more severe
forms of panic disorder, obsessive compulsive disorder and

social phobia into the category of serious mental disorder (Andrews 1994). This is not to say people with severe disorders have a serious mental illness. Rather it is the recognition of the extreme disablement caused through the disorders. I will discuss the secondary conditions in detail in the following chapter.

Minimization and prevention

Almost everyone I have been in contact with brings up this point: 'If only I had known what was wrong from the beginning. If only I knew from the beginning how to deal with it. The rest— the secondary conditions—would never have happened'. To minimize the disorders and prevent the secondary conditions an accurate diagnosis and appropriate treatment is needed from the outset. A lack of diagnosis and/or inappropriate treatment leaves the way open for the development of the disorders and the secondary conditions.

Causes

Except in the case of post traumatic stress disorder, the causes of other anxiety disorders are still unknown. The disorders usually begin during or after a major life stress, or a period of continual stress. Much of the research has centered on panic disorder, and various theories have been suggested.

Physiological research suggests a chemical imbalance may be involved, although researchers are unsure whether any chemical imbalance is the cause, or a result of, the panic attack. Behavior theories consider that anxiety disorders are learned behaviors and recovery means unlearning the previous limiting behavior. Psychoanalytic theory postulates that anxiety stems from sub-conscious unresolved conflicts which began during childhood. It is possible that the three schools of thought are each partly correct, and viewed together they form a whole picture of cause and effect (APA 1990).

Another theory currently being investigated is the role dis-sociation plays in anxiety disorders. Putman (1989) suggests that dissociative phenomena exist on a continuum' and range from 'a normal process' through to the most severe, dissociative identity disorder, which is the experience of separate multiple selves.

· **Dissociation can also be described as altered or discrete**
· **states of consciousness, or trance states. Dissociated states**

include: depersonalization, the experience of being detached or out of the body; derealization where ourselves and/or our surroundings do not seem real, as if we are looking through a white or grey mist; a sensation that our body has expanded or conversely has shrunk; feelings of floating, or of falling into a void; stationary objects appearing to move; and intolerance to light and/or sound.

From what I have found over the years, the ability to dissociate is very common in people who experience spontaneous panic attacks. It is interesting to note that once people who dissociate have an understanding of the phenomena, they report the experience of dissociation as being the trigger for the panic attack. Current research suggests the 'sleep' panic attack occurs 'during the transition from stage two to stage three sleep' (Uhde 1994). In other words, during an alteration of consciousness. I will discuss dissociation in more detail in chapter five.

Whatever the ultimate cause, people can still learn how to control the disorder naturally, without the use of medications. Learning how to control it means learning how to manage it without fear and panic. Unresolved childhood issues can also play a major role for people who experience anxiety disorders. Such issues need to be addressed and resolved.

Personal and socio-economic costs

The extent of the disabilities people suffer through the disorders mean that we, as a community, lose the many and varied talents of these people. Not only is there a horrific personal cost, there is also an enormous socio-economic cost to the community.

In 1980 the economic cost of panic disorder, calculated in terms of employment losses, disability benefits, financial support and health care costs, was estimated at US $1 billion.

After speaking with over 12 000 people with an anxiety disorder, I have no doubt in my mind we are the most medically tested group of people in the country. In an effort to find out what is wrong we may see a number of doctors and specialists. We can undergo a range of medical tests including cardiographs, brain scans, testing for ulcers, numerous blood tests, not once but at least twice if not three, four or more times. As our symptoms can be unremitting we may regularly seek professional help either through our doctor or by attending the casualty department of our local public hospital.

Unfortunately this can be to no avail. Without a diagnosis and appropriate treatment many people become so disabled through the disorders they are forced to give up their jobs and rely on social security benefits. Others may refuse a job promotion or may need to take a lower paid position in an effort to cope with their disorder.

The cost to the community through these disorders is still not acknowledged, let alone addressed. Health care costs are soaring, yet many of the costs could be lessened through understanding and relevant treatment. Anxiety disorders and the secondary conditions are treatable. People can recover and resume normal lives. Greater awareness and understanding within the health professions and the general community will lessen both the personal and monetary costs.

CASE HISTORIES

Anne

Anne was thirty when she had her first panic attack. She was driving to the office where she worked as a secretary. She had just pulled up at a set of traffic lights when for no apparent reason she felt an 'electric shock' go right through her body, which reacted to the powerful tingling surge. Anne's heart began to race and she had difficulty breathing. A wave of nausea followed, and her hands and legs began to tremble. She felt she was looking down at herself as if she had left her body. Everything appeared unreal. All Anne could think of was that she was dying, and she panicked.

Tom

It was 1.00 am. Tom had been asleep since 11.00 pm. He was due to return to his teaching position the next day, after two weeks school holidays. Tom woke with a start as his body jerked violently. A surge of heat went through him. His heart was pounding and he was gasping for breath. His shoulders and arms began to ache and he felt as if he were going to faint. Tom woke his wife, who then called an ambulance as they both feared he was having a heart attack.

Elizabeth

Elizabeth closed the door to the children's room and walked into the living room. It had been a long day and she was looking forward to being able to relax. A tingling feeling went through her and it felt as if her heart missed a couple of beats. She felt as if 'a volume control' had been turned up in her head, as the sound from the television and the cars in the street began to seem intolerably loud. The floor seemed to move up and down. Elizabeth began to experience pins and needles in her arms and feet. She was frightened by what was happening to her. She was alone with the children and her husband was not due home for another hour. Her fear intensified.

The family

Partners and family members are also considerably disadvantaged by the lack of understanding. Obviously, being able to understand the disorder and its implications is very important for everyone involved. It is difficult and frustrating because it seems that we won't 'pull ourselves together'. The disruption to the family because we can't 'pull ourselves together' is an ongoing source of guilt and shame for many people.

It can help if our partner or family members can talk with other people who are in the same situation. This mutual support can be very beneficial. Self-help groups usually encourage partners and family members to attend programs or group meetings, which can alleviate some of the distress and helplessness many partners and family members feel.

Talking with a therapist may also help, whether it is our therapist or a different one. There may be occasions where family therapy would be useful, and again this can be done by our therapist or another.

Some partners or family members may want to become actively involved in our recovery. This can be extremely worthwhile. Being involved with a self-help group or a therapist, or both, can help partners or family members understand exactly what is involved. Being involved helps to balance the excessive pressure or over-protectiveness of some partners or family members.

Guilt and shame

We all feel ashamed and guilty about the effect on our family. Despite these feelings, we need to be careful because we can unintentionally create further disruption. Many of us feel we need to have someone with us at all times. This can be very reassuring for us, but we need to make sure we do not restrict the lives of people around us. Until we are able to manage on our own, it is a matter of finding a balance which will answer our needs and the needs of our family.

The guilt and shame sometimes mean we isolate ourselves from our partner or family in an attempt not to cause further worry and grief. Many of us do not realize how devastating this can be for them. If they want to help, don't shut them out because of guilt and shame.

Unfortunately, the reverse can also happen and we may find our partner or family isolates us. Although we may feel like giving up completely, we mustn't. We may also feel as if we will never be able to do it without them. We can. Being involved with a self-help group enables us to make contact with other people who are in a similar position. Their support and encouragement can help us to begin to rebuild our lives. Despite the seemingly impossible obstacles, we can all recover.

Chapter 3

Secondary conditions

The attacks

Everyone who experiences spontaneous panic attack remembers their first attack: where they were, what they were doing and how they felt. There is no other experience with which to compare it. The panic attack usually appears to have little or nothing to do with any personal or environmental situation. Even if we are very distressed about a particular situation it can seem to us there is no direct relationship between the situation and the attack. Whereas in social phobia, obsessive compulsive disorder and post traumatic stress disorder, people may recognize the driving force behind their attack as it is usually specific to a particular situation.

Most people who experience a spontaneous attack will go straight to a doctor or the nearest hospital, sometimes by ambulance, as the attack feels as if it is actually a heart attack. We go through the standard clinical tests which show there is nothing physically wrong. Many of us are now diagnosed as suffering from a panic attack, although a large number of people are still only told they are suffering from stress or anxiety.

There is no relief in discovering that there is nothing physically wrong. The attack can be so severe and the physical reaction so extreme, it is difficult to believe there is not a physical cause. It is impossible not to feel frightened, especially if there appears to be little or no relationship between the panic attack and our current personal situation.

The primary fears

The primary fears are usually established from the first panic attack. The first and most common fear is 'I'm having a heart attack' and/or 'I am going to die'. The second is 'I am going insane', and the third is 'I'm going to lose control of myself' which could mean 'I'm going to faint'; 'I'm going to make a fool of myself'; 'I will vomit'; 'I will have an attack of diarrhea'; or, literally, 'I am going to lose control'.

From the primary fears come flow-on fears. In the past much attention was given to the flow-on fears—what we can and cannot do—and in the past treatment was usually aimed at them instead of the cause—the spontaneous panic attacks.

CASE HISTORIES

Susan

Susan called her husband at work and asked him to come home because she was frightened something was going to happen to her. She had been to five different doctors and not one of them could tell her what was wrong with her. Most had said she was just anxious, and had prescribed various tranquilizers and other medications. She couldn't make them understand that she knew she was anxious. Feeling the way she did was making her anxious. If they could just tell her what was wrong with her and help her she would stop being anxious. It was beginning to affect her relationship with her husband. She didn't want to bother him at work, but she didn't know what else to do.

Paul

Paul sat on the side of the hospital bed. He was being discharged after a night in hospital for observation because he felt as if he were having a heart attack. The specialist had told him he had not had a heart attack, but a panic attack. Paul had tried to tell the specialist that of course he had panicked. He had felt terrible and thought he was going to die. Surely, he thought, it was normal to panic under those circumstances.

Julie

The end of Julie's shift was in sight. Another hour and she could go home, but first she had to hand over to the nurses on afternoon shift. She felt her stomach tighten and her anxiety increase. Julie had never had problems talking in front of other people before but the thought of hand-over today terrified her. She remembered the last few weeks and how it had become increasingly difficult for her to appear 'normal'. Julie had had her first panic attack at work. Although she knew what was wrong with her, she was having enormous difficulty trying to 'pull herself together'. She couldn't control what was happening to her. She knew the other nurses wouldn't understand if they found out. Julie felt she couldn't go to any of the doctors at the hospital where she worked, as she was frightened they would make her resign.

Belinda

It was Saturday night and Belinda was at home with her parents. Her friends were out celebrating the end of their first year at university. They hadn't been able to understand when Belinda pulled out of university during the second semester. She had always been a straight A student. Now she wasn't doing anything at all. She refused all invitations to go out and stayed at home most of the time. She went out only occasionally with her parents. Her brother had told her friends that one of their parents had to be with her at all times because she was continually frightened of being alone.

Sam

Sam drove his truck out of the depot and onto the road that would take him to the freeway. He wiped the perspiration from his forehead. His hands were trembling. He had to keep going. This time he couldn't go back to the depot and say he was sick. Once more and he knew he would lose his job. His stomach was churning. The further away he was from the depot the worse he became. All Sam wanted to do was go home. He didn't know how much more he could take. Over the last twelve months he had stopped doing most of the things he used to enjoy, playing or watching sport, having a few drinks with friends or going for a drive with his family. Now he just stayed at home. It took all his energy just to get to work and get through each day.

Michael

Michael had been on stress leave for eight weeks and was due to return to work. He had spoken to his rehabilitation counselor because his condition, far from easing, was becoming worse. Since being on leave his panic attacks had increased and his anxiety level was very high. Every time he left the familiar surroundings of his neighborhood he would be overcome with the fear of having another panic attack. More often than not he would have one. The consulting doctor had said Michael was just suffering from stress and that he should think seriously about 'getting his act together' and getting back to work. After all, said the doctor, Michael was lucky to have a job to go back to. No one seemed to understand that all Michael wanted to do was return to work. He certainly didn't like what was happening to him. He had always been conscientious at work and had rarely taken time off. He wondered if he should resign. He thought it would be better than having to face the doubts of his counselor and doctor.

The what ifs

Getting a diagnosis with an inadequate, or no explanation, brings feelings of unease and disquiet. From these, the 'what ifs' are born. 'What if the doctor has made a mistake?' 'What if there is really something wrong which has been overlooked?'. Our fear pushes the anxiety level higher and we do have another panic attack. The cycle of panic and anxiety has begun. We can't imagine why, if we are only suffering from stress or anxiety, we can't 'pull ourselves together'. In fact, the harder we try, the worse we become.

The lack of understanding

The various treatments we try are either partially effective or completely ineffective. The responsibility is thrown onto us. We are not trying to 'pull ourselves together', we are 'obviously getting something out of being this way', we are 'weak and have no will power' or 'no strength of character'.

Ineffective treatment does not mean we are ineffective people. The lack of understanding and inadequate treatment does make it appear to everyone, including family, friends and doctors that we can't 'pull ourselves together'. But what everyone doesn't realize is that if it were so easy, we would have 'pulled ourselves together' long before now. Many of us are living with anxiety and panic attacks as constant companions, and the fear of what is happening to us can't be brushed aside or dismissed so easily.

Without adequate understanding and treatment we do not know how to effectively control what is happening to us, so we use other forms of control in an effort to ease our situation. Ironically and tragically, many of the controls we use actually become the secondary conditions and help to compound and perpetuate the disorder. This in turn perpetuates and compounds the myth that we are not doing anything to help ourselves.

Agoraphobia—avoidance behavior

Agoraphobia is one such control. Developing agoraphobia has meant a lifetime of limitation for many people. Until the recognition of panic disorder as a separate condition in 1980, agoraphobia was considered to be a primary condition. Treatment was focused on it, instead of the disorder.

Agoraphobia used to be defined as fear of open spaces. In panic disorder, agoraphobia is now recognized as 'anxiety about being in situations or places from which escape might be difficult or embarrassing, or in which help may not be available in the event of having an uncued or situationally predisposed attack', and/or 'the situation is endured with marked distress or anxiety ... or may require the presence of a companion' (APA 1994).

Agoraphobia in Social Phobia is avoidance behavior 'limited to' social situations. In obsessive compulsive disorder it is avoidance behavior relating to the particular obsessive thoughts and in post traumatic stress disorder it is avoidance of 'stimuli' related to the trauma (APA 1994). Although the avoidance behavior is limited to the particular disorder, it can be all encompassing and people may become housebound.

Some people will become housebound, totally avoiding situations and/or places, from the first spontaneous attack. In other cases, avoidance behavior may be gradual and increasingly restricting, or it may be permanently limited to one or two situations and/or places. People may have occasional panic attacks for years before avoidance behavior sets in. In this case, the onset of avoidance behavior is not a result of the panic attack itself, but is usually a fear of a new symptom of anxiety.

> **Agoraphobia can affect people in different degrees. It can also affect the same person in different degrees at different times. It is a multi-faceted and multi-contradictory condition.**

Avoidance behavior doesn't mean we are not trying to 'pull ourselves together', nor does it mean we are giving in to the disorder. Avoidance behavior is a defense against it, and it has been one of the few controls we've had.

An overall defense

Avoidance behavior can be divided into three different categories. The first category is the avoidance of situations and/or places as an overall defense against further anxiety and panic attacks. Avoidance behavior, either partial or total, does not necessarily mean a cessation of anxiety or panic attacks. For many of us it can mean relative safety and most importantly, privacy.

The development of avoidance behavior means everyday normal situations and/or places can become associated with anxiety and panic attacks. Although we are not frightened of the particular situation or place, we avoid them as an ongoing defense or control of anxiety and panic attacks.

We begin to become restricted in where we can and can't go. We may find we can travel within a certain radius of a few miles of home, and do everything we normally do in relative comfort and safety. Once outside these invisible boundaries our anxiety soars. As an overall control of the disorder, we stay within these invisible boundaries. This may mean becoming restricted not only to the house, but to one room. Even then the anxiety and panic attacks can still remain.

Avoidance behavior can be very subtle and gradual, as the area of relative safety diminishes over time. We are able to do some things one day, only to find ourselves unable to do them the next. Although it appears illogical to others, this defense against panic attacks and anxiety can mean a possible reduction in them. The cost of this defense is high, as it can mean a total breakdown of our previous lifestyle.

Anticipatory anxiety

The second category of avoidance behavior is caused through anticipatory anxiety, the 'what ifs'. This category differs from the first in its defense and control. The first category is an overall, ongoing attempt to control the disorder; the second is a defense against a specific spiral of high anxiety.

Anticipatory anxiety is the fear of having a panic attack while meeting a specific commitment. The overall defense against ongoing anxiety and panic attacks sometimes reduces them to a manageable level. However, the relative safety is lost when we have to break through our invisible boundaries to meet a specific commitment. It can be caused by going to the local shop, going out with family or friends, or anything.

It doesn't matter if the event is five minutes or five months away. The anticipation of having to go past our invisible boundaries means breaking our tenuous control of our overall defense. This triggers the 'what ifs': 'what if I can't do it?' 'what if I do have a panic attack?'. By the time we have to leave home to meet the commitment the anxiety level may be so high we cancel our plans and stay home. In other words, we *avoid* because of a specific spiral of anxiety.

Feeling unwell

The third category of avoidance behavior is not known or realized by almost anyone who does not have the disorder. It is the avoidance of situations and/or places because of feeling generally unwell most of the time.

As well as suffering the symptoms of anxiety and panic attacks, our level of overall fitness deteriorates rapidly. We begin to experience a general sense of feeling unwell. Some people compare this to ongoing 'flu-like' symptoms. We are also continually exhausted, as the anxiety and panic attacks consume all our energy. Going out, going to work or doing the normal day-to-day things around the house mean not only trying to keep the anxiety and panic attacks at bay, but also trying to overcome the feeling of being unwell and the all-consuming fatigue.

Alcohol

The use of alcohol is another control and some people will go on to develop an alcohol dependence. Both men and women use it, although it appears to be the major control used by men.

Many people with the disorders feel it is more socially acceptable to have an alcohol problem than to admit to having an anxiety disorder. The symptoms of a hangover can also perpetuate the anxiety. We misinterpret these symptoms as a warning of an impending panic attack, so we have another drink in an effort to control it.

Medication

Drugs are another control people use. The risk of dependence on drugs is well researched. Medication is one of the main treatments for the disorder, yet the anxiety and panic attacks can blast through our 'chemical calm'. In many cases the dosage is increased, either by ourselves or by our doctor. When attempts are made to withdraw from the medication, anxiety and panic attacks can return in full force, along with withdrawal symptoms. In an effort to stop the increased anxiety, panic attacks and symptoms of withdrawal, some people will continue with the medication and become trapped in the cycle of dependence.

Depression

With little or no effective treatment many people may develop a major depression in reaction to their disorder. Until recently this depression was also seen as a primary condition. Although steps were taken to treat the depression, the primary cause—the anxiety disorder—was rarely considered, let alone treated.

Suicide

The disintegration of ourselves and our lives through the disorder and its secondary conditions brings a sense of hopelessness and helplessness. Suddenly, and in major contradiction to the fear of dying, we may find ourselves contemplating or attempting suicide. It begins to appear as the only way out. It is not.

Part of the danger of this development is that most of us will not discuss it with family members or our doctor. The sense of 'this is not me', and the shame and humiliation which we feel, counteract our most desperate plea for help. Most of us would never have considered ourselves as ever being suicidal. The realization we are even considering suicide only causes further fear and confusion, which in turn isolates us even further. If we do find ourselves thinking of suicide, it is very important we seek professional help. Suicide is not the answer. Recovery is—and we can recover with appropriate treatment.

CASE HISTORIES

Bill

Bill walked from his manager's office. He knew the day would come when he would be found out and today was that day. He had been caught drinking during working hours in the bar of the hotel, a few doors down from the office. He had been a regular visitor to the hotel, as he made his daily courier rounds to the head office, a few blocks away. Having a drink was the way he had found to help him cope with the panic attacks and perpetual anxiety. Bill had a regular routine. A drink before going to work, one during his morning round, two at lunch, one on the afternoon round and two before he drove home. He felt he had at least one thing in his favor. The manager didn't know about his anxiety problem. Bill thought that having a drinking problem was much more socially acceptable than having an anxiety problem. What Bill didn't know was that his manager also had the same anxiety disorder!

Patricia

The prescription lay on the table. Will she or won't she have it filled? Years ago Patricia had been given a similar medication. She had never liked the thought of taking it, but the panic attacks and the anxiety finally convinced her she had to do something. It had helped for a while, but over time she found she had to keep increasing the dose for it to have any effect. Finally she decided enough was enough, and slowly withdrew from the medication. Patricia had learnt to cope with the panic attacks and the anxiety, but over the last two months they had become more and more intense. She didn't want to take the medication, but as no one could suggest any other way of controling the disorder she felt as if there were no alternative.

Robyn

Robyn looked at her mother in silence. It was no use, her mother was never going to understand that Robyn's panic disorder was a legitimate condition and that Robyn was not just being 'stupid'. Her cousin also had panic disorder/agoraphobia and had committed suicide a month before. No one had known until after his death exactly what had been wrong with him. He had never told anyone outside his immediate family. Yet Robyn's mother still would not be convinced. She told Robyn that the family was not the type to have this sort of problem and that she had better 'pull herself together' and stop being so ridiculous.

Self absorption

Self absorption, an experience of being turned inward and preoccupied with oneself, is another control against anxiety and panic attacks. It does not form the basis of one of the secondary conditions, but is one of the ways we try to control the unexpected. Ironically, for those of us who dissociate, it could contribute to our primary disorder, because this kind of inner concentration can trigger an out-of-body sensation (depersonalization) or other kind of detached feelings (i.e. derealization), which I have noticed is often a precursor to a panic attack.

This control again makes it seem to family and friends that we are continually dwelling on the problem. We are, but not in the way it appears. We can become totally self absorbed and, more often than not, we will be accused of being selfish. Most of us would probably agree, but at this stage there is not much we can do about it.

Most of us who develop the disorder would consider ourselves as having been extroverts before it's onset. As the anxiety and the panic attacks take hold, we become extremely introverted and self absorbed. Our preoccupation is extremely exasperating to others in the family.

To understand this control we all need to be aware that everyone who suffers from the disorder, particularly those who are beginning to develop secondary conditions, are caught in an ever-growing maze of anxiety, panic attacks and fear. There appears to be nothing we, or anyone, can do to stop it. The result of this is completely devastating. Our whole life, as we have known it, begins to disintegrate around us.

Under the circumstances it is completely normal and natural to become preoccupied. The preoccupation is a means of trying to find a way out of our distress. We are trying to find an answer to what appear to be unanswerable questions.

The preoccupation is also part of the monitoring process. Monitoring each symptom is another way of defending against it. By continually monitoring symptoms we hope to gain advanced warning of a panic attack. Although we are not sure how, we feel there might be time to stop panic attack, or at least to get help before anything happens.

There is much truth in the statement that by 'dwelling on something only makes it worse'. With an anxiety disorder, not dwelling on it is almost impossible. We feel as if our lives are in constant danger, so it is difficult not to think about it.

The need to be in control

There is another control, which actually forms the basis of all the other controls we use. It can be so subtle that many of us may not be aware of it. It is the need to be in control, not only of ourselves but of our whole environment.

The need to be in control permeates every aspect of our life. We feel we need to be in control as we have already lost so much to the disorder. We are afraid of what might happen if we lose control.

Most of us have never been aware of the need to be in control, but it has always been part of us, long before the onset of the disorder. As a result of the disorder, this control becomes paramount. Our sense of helplessness and fear demand nothing less. When the anxiety and panic attacks break away from this control we feel even more helpless than before.

> **The need to be in control is the main obstacle towards recovery. Recovery means the opposite. Recovery means we need to let go of the need to be in control. We don't realize our overwhelming need to be in control perpetuates our disorder.**

There are many various aspects to this particular control, which are discussed in detail later. To let go of this control is unimaginable, but letting go means recovery, and with recovery comes freedom.

Chapter 4

Therapies

The number of therapies and treatments which people have tried with little or no result is a major area of concern. Not only does this contribute to the general sense of helplessness and hopelessness, it can also generate anger towards the health professions. In some cases this will prevent people from seeking further help.

Before we look at why various treatments haven't been as effective as they could have been, we will look at the issue of anger.

Understanding our anger

In many instances our anger is more than justified, but we need to realize why we haven't had the help we need. We also need to be careful that our anger doesn't prevent us from seeking further help.

We may be angry about the overall lack of understanding and knowledge of anxiety disorders, or at not receiving an earlier diagnosis and effective treatment. Many people who have had the disorder for years feel cheated by the loss of family, social and employment opportunities. There is also anger that the lack of understanding has strengthened the myths and stigma surrounding anxiety disorders. These myths include: we are weak in character, not trying hard enough, or gaining too many secondary benefits from the disorder to really want to recover.

We need to understand why adequate help has not been available to us, and why it is still limited. As I said in the beginning, panic disorder has only been classified as a separate disorder since 1980. It has been only in the last few years that researchers have realized the possible serious disabilities associated with the disorders. Up until now the lack of understanding and adequate treatment hasn't been anyone's fault. The community as a whole is still not aware of the full extent and possible serious disabilities associated with the disorders; as individuals, we are. Some of us live with the disorder for years, but because of the lack of understanding we are too ashamed and humiliated to speak out. This is a mistake.

The need to be perfect

Prior to the disorder, many of us were perfectionists and, despite the disorder, many of us still try to present this image. Not only have we tried to be the perfect partner, the perfect parent, the perfect employee or employer, but we become the perfect patient. Discussing issues where we feel ashamed or humiliated does not fit our 'perfect' image, so we hold back.

Being open and honest

In many instances we will not tell our doctor or therapist the full effects of what we are experiencing, including our thoughts of suicide. We cannot receive the help we need unless we are being completely open.

Even if we are being completely open, our need to be perfect hides our feelings of inadequacy. Many of us accept inadequate treatment because we feel inadequate. We feel we don't have the right to complain, then we become angry because we don't receive the help we need.

In some cases there can be misguided loyalties to the doctor, therapist or our family. Although we complain privately, we continue to go to back to our doctor or therapist because we feel we don't want to let our family, doctor or therapist down.

In some cases family members feel a stronger loyalty to the therapist than we do. The family pressures us to remain with the therapist, so we stay in a therapy situation which may be of little benefit. Our sense of inadequacy keeps us from speaking out.

Our silence

Not only do we live in fear of the disorder, we live in fear of other people knowing we have it. Many of us live in silence in case our employer, friends and family find out. This silence is passed on from generation to generation. As we begin to understand our disorder, many of us realize that one of our parents or other family members also has the disorder. Sometimes, tragically, when our parents or other family members became aware that the disorder was beginning to develop in the next generation, they remained silent, just as many of us are now doing.

This silence needs to be broken. Anxiety disorders directly affect millions of people and indirectly affect families, friends, employers and the community as a whole. Together we have an enormous voice which can help to speed up the changes needed in the health care system.

CASE HISTORIES

Wendy

Wendy was convinced she would never recover. She had had the disorder for twenty-five years, and during that time she had seen many doctors, psychiatrists and psychologists, taken all types of medication and even spent six months in a private hospital, all to little or no avail. She had never been told exactly what was wrong with her, although a doctor had told her she was depressed. She thought it was natural that, feeling the way she did, she was depressed, and wondered why people treated only her depression and not the panic attacks. At the hospital her doctor and the nurses would pat her on the shoulder and tell her to 'think positive'. She tried, but it was difficult when her life had disintegrated and there seemed no way she could ever get back to 'normal'. After leaving the hospital she refused to see any other doctor or specialist. She was angry and frustrated at the lack of help, but there appeared to be no solution. Gradually Wendy was able to arrange her life around the disorder. She could do her own shopping at the local store, but she spent most of her time at home. Her children grew up with the impression that their mother was a bit 'odd', but they accepted her as she was and never questioned her decision not to seek further help.

Darryl

Darryl's session with his psychiatrist had not gone well. What had started off as a normal session ended with the psychiatrist telling Darryl that as he had made so much improvement, his sessions could be cut back to once a month. Darryl knew he had made a mistake and he walked out of the psychiatrist's office feeling totally devastated. What his psychiatrist didn't know was that Darryl was in fact worse than when he first started seeing the psychiatrist. Two weeks ago Darryl had refused a promotion, as he was already having difficulty with his current job. He had begun to think suicide was his only solution. Darryl thought back to all the times when he wasn't completely open with his psychiatrist. He hadn't wanted to explain all the details of what he was experiencing, as he had never met anyone who really understood what was happening to him. He didn't think this psychiatrist would be any different. Darryl was also afraid that if he told the psychiatrist everything, he would have been committed to a psychiatric hospital. Darryl wondered if he should ring the psychiatrist and explain everything, but he felt too humiliated and ashamed.

Jackie

Jackie and her husband had spent the evening talking about their son, who was experiencing ongoing panic attacks and was now too frightened to go to school. The school had threatened them with legal action if he did not return to school the following week. The parents were given two options on how to get him there: either a teacher would be sent to collect him and, once at school, would stand over him all day to ensure he remained at school; or, to cure him of his fear, the teacher would take him to a nearby town and leave him there to find his own way back. When he got back he would see there was nothing to be frightened of. Jackie had explained to the school and her husband about the panic disorder. Although her husband tried to understand, the school couldn't. Jackie had tried to comfort her son and to help him in whatever way she could, but her son had told her she didn't really understand. She did. Jackie had developed panic disorder after her son's birth but she had never told anyone, not even her husband. Jackie felt she couldn't tell anyone even now.

What we can do

The anger many of us feel can be used in a positive and constructive way. When we direct our anger towards the disorder instead of ourselves, it can be the 'rocketship' towards recovery. I will discuss this further in chapter five.

We can also use our anger to help bring about changes to the health care system. If we are being completely open with our doctor or therapist, and they don't know or want to understand, then we need to find someone who does. In the past this was not easy, but the situation is changing and will continue to change if we break our silence.

While we may still not wish to tell employers and friends, there are still other things we can do. We can write letters to the governing bodies of the various health professions and to the local state and federal agencies. Local self-help groups or the Consumer Health Advocacy agencies in each state are also available for advice and support. Individually we live in silence. Together we can break it.

Most importantly, our anger must not prevent us from seeking help. Understanding why various therapies haven't worked will help us understand what will.

Therapies

Many of us go from one therapy to another, only to find ourselves ending where we started. Although the panic attacks and anxiety may diminish for a while, they come back, sometimes worse than before.

Irrespective of how many therapies we have tried, the overall lack of understanding means that most of us have never been taught how to manage our disorder ourselves. Most treatments not only fail to teach management skills, they usually only treat one particular aspect of the disorder. The disorder and its secondary conditions need to be treated as a whole, not in isolation.

It is important for all of us to understand that although various therapies have not worked by themselves, when they are used together they can become extremely powerful tools for recovery.

Medication

Medication, particularly tranquilizers, has been one of the first defenses against panic attacks and anxiety. In many cases it has been the only form of treatment we have received. Even if a miracle drug for anxiety and panic attacks became available, I wonder how many people would want to take it permanently? From what I have been told over the years of people's intense dislike of taking any form of medication, I don't think many people would.

People with anxiety disorders report becoming very sensitive, not only to light and sound, but their whole state of being becomes very sensitive. It is not unusual for people with panic disorder to develop allergies which they didn't have before the onset of the disorder. This sensitivity can be quite acute, so it is advisable to be aware of it and to be careful when taking any medications, including herbal or other preparations bought over the counter.

Tranquilizers

Although tranquilizers were one of the first defenses against anxiety, the growing controversy over their use for some of the anxiety disorders means this type of treatment is slowly being withdrawn. The current trend is not to prescribe tranquilizers for anxiety disorders. If they are prescribed, then it is only for a two to four week period (Brayley et al. 1991). While this will lower the risk of possible addiction, it does not solve the original difficulties caused through the limited understanding, treatment facilities and resources for people with anxiety disorders.

We are all aware of the millions of prescriptions written each year for tranquilizers, which in itself should be enough to highlight this problem in the community. It hasn't. The controversy over tranquilizers should have added further emphasis. It hasn't. We need to be taught management skills from the beginning. This would enable us to take control of our disorder from the outset.

People who have been taking tranquilizers over a long period of time are in a similar situation. Although there are withdrawal programs, there is still only limited help available. Again, management skills need to be taught and they can be of great assistance during any withdrawal process.

Anti-depressants

Anti-depressants are now becoming widely used in the treatment of panic disorder/agoraphobia, with varying degrees of success in keeping the anxiety and the panic attacks at bay. While anti-depressants are very important in helping to contain any reactive depression, they do not teach the necessary management skills. When medication is used, it should be in conjunction with other therapies.

- **As most people do not like taking medication of any sort, it is not unusual for people to simply stop taking it. This may have serious consequences. Withdrawal from any medication must be done under medical supervision.**

Withdrawal

Withdrawal from medication, including anti-depressants, may mean a return of high levels of anxiety and panic attacks, and some of us may experience other symptoms of withdrawal. Withdrawal must be done under the supervision of a doctor. Cognitive behavioral techniques have been found to assist in withdrawal from tranquilizers and high success rates for withdrawal using these techniques have now been demonstrated (Otto et al. 1994). There are tranquilizer support groups in some states who can help to support us during this phase of our recovery. But remember, withdrawal must be done under medical supervision.

- **Medication, in any form, takes control and power away from us. It doesn't teach us the necessary skills to gain control over our lives. In some cases it is necessary in the short term, but it is not a long-term answer.**

Cognitive behavioral therapy: CBT

We control every aspect of our life except the way we think, yet it is our thinking which is also a major contributor to the perpetuation of the disorders. Many of us are aware of the predominant role our thoughts do play. This was confirmed in one Australian study of panic disorder that showed patients had 'a clear bias toward attributing cause to cognitive factors'(Kenardy et al. 1988). That is: patients were very clear in their opinions that their thoughts caused much of their distress. As in my experience with clients, the study also showed people preferred 'cognitive coping strategies' in preference to medication. Yet without professional assistance many of us are unable to break the cycle of anxiety producing thoughts.

> **We continually add to our fear by the way we think. In other words we are continually scaring ourselves with our thoughts.**

CBT is a series of strategies specifically targeted to our particular disorder. For panic disorder these strategies can include relaxation, breathing techniques and 'interoceptive exposure' and cognitive therapy. This is usually conducted by a trained cognitive behavioral therapist and is usually done in the therapist's office. This is called *in vivo*.

Interoceptive exposure is designed to produce a number of the most common symptoms, including accelerated heart rate, dizziness and the effects of hyperventilation. Combined with cognitive techniques we can begin to change our fearful interpretation of the symptoms and break the anxiety producing thoughts. Armed with cognitive behavioral strategies we go into situations and/or places and 'test' our ability to manage our anxiety and panic attacks.

People who have overlapping symptoms of other anxiety disorders need to be taught the various cognitive behavioral strategies related to each symptom group. Studies indicate that short-term CBT can have lasting beneficial effects (Otto et al. 1994). Unfortunately CBT has not been readily available, although this situation is beginning to change.

Graded exposure

Many people were, and still are, being given a graded exposure program as treatment for their agoraphobia. Along with medication this may be the only other form of treatment people have received. Graded exposure does not cover the many strategies used in CBT and is simply exposure to situations and/ or places we avoid.

The question many people with panic disorder/agoraphobia ask is, 'exposure to what'? Many graded exposure programs treat the avoidance behavior in panic disorder as though it was the situation or place which triggered the attack. Much to their confusion, people who have panic disorders without any form of avoidance behavior have been, or are given, a graded exposure program.

The rationale behind graded exposure programs is that when people put themselves into avoided situations/or places and stay in that situation or place, then the anxiety and/or panic attack will peak and slowly ebb away. In other words the person will habituate to the anxiety and panic attack in that situation or place. As many people say, even though the panic attack does subside, if they are not directly frightened of the situation/or place why would the anxiety 'ebb away' when it has never done so before.

> **Trying to correct avoidance behavior without working on the cause means limited success, which can be destroyed by the next panic attack.**

Most of these programs insist people stay in the situation or place until the anxiety and panic attack subsides and this is also one of the main complaints from people with panic disorder. It seems illogical to stay in a city mall (or any other place) for hours on end in an effort to reduce anxiety. Many are chronically anxious day-in, day-out, and are also experiencing ongoing panic attacks. As people say, if they were going to habituate to the anxiety and the panic attacks they would have already done so, irrespective of where they were.

To compound the issue and the confusion, many panic disorder clients are asked to list their secondary fears and a graded exposure program is built around them. In some cases the list of fears included specific fears which pre-dated the attacks and have no bearing on the disorder, yet they are incorporated or become the main feature of the exposure program. This little known but crucial fact has also been noted by researchers. One such study showed, 'half the simple (specific) phobias in panic disorder had childhood onset and half had onset associated with the onset of panic disorder' (Argyle et al. 1990).

The new categories of panic attacks demonstrate quite clearly the spontaneous panic attack is triggered by internal cues not external ones. In panic disorder, treatment needs to be aimed at these internal cues.

CASE HISTORIES

Melissa

Melissa had a part-time job and had to work at night. On most nights she was alone, except for customers coming and going. Melissa was scared of being held up, as there was always quite a bit of cash around. Her fear increased and her anxiety became all-pervasive. She decided to seek help and was put on a three-month waiting list to see a therapist. During this time her anxiety and fear escalated. Melissa felt she had no alternative but to resign, but her fear and anxiety continued. When she finally saw the therapist she filled out various forms and spoke to the therapist about her fears. The next time she saw him she noticed a jar of spiders on his desk. Melissa asked him about them and he replied that as she was also scared of spiders, the first step was to confront her fear of them. The therapist then left the office leaving her with the spiders. Melissa had always been scared of spiders; she could not remember a time when she wasn't. She didn't care about her fear of spiders, but here she was sitting in an office looking at a jar of them. All she wanted to do was to stop the anxiety so she could go back to work. She walked out and didn't go back.

Cynthia

Cynthia had panic disorder but didn't avoid anything. She went to work and did everything she had to do, but it was very difficult. She went to see a specialist, although she had to wait five months for an appointment. When she got there he was three hours late. He finally arrived, but didn't apologize for keeping her waiting. Although Cynthia had an hour appointment, it only lasted for twenty minutes. She told the specialist about the panic attacks and he kept asking her what she was scared of. Cynthia kept telling him she was always scared and anxious that she might die from the attacks. The specialist kept saying she had to be scared of something and Cynthia wasn't sure what he was getting at. In the end she said she had always been scared of elevators, but that was long before the panic attacks started. The specialist told her to go into the foyer and get into an elevator and go up and down in it until her anxiety disappeared. With that he finished the appointment and told her to book another with his secretary. She was so confused and angry she never went back.

Alice, Toni, Carlie

Alice asked the local discussion group what she should do about her therapist, who always went to sleep during her appointments. Toni and Carlie looked at her and told her their therapists always went to sleep too. It didn't take long for them to realize they were talking about the same therapist. When the group asked them why they didn't speak to him about it or try and find another therapist, the three of them said he was obviously very tired and they didn't want to hurt his feelings.

Psychotherapy

Psychotherapy has sometimes been the only treatment people have tried. If you have had the misfortune to go to a therapist who is unresponsive or uninformed about the nature of anxiety disorders, it can be difficult to trust that therapy may be helpful. You may even believe psychotherapy is irrelevant to your problem. However, the right therapist can be a significant ally in your healing process, and you should persevere until you find someone you trust to understand you. And if you believe you may have a history of child abuse or have undergone some other trauma in your life, psychotherapy is vitally important.

Despite the sense of shame many of us feel over these issues, trauma must be dealt with for our long-term well-being. There are very understanding and caring therapists working in the area of childhood abuse. There are referral agencies in every state for psychiatrists, psychologists, marriage and family counselors and social workers, many of whom have special training in this field. Many neighborhoods have mental health centers and regional counseling agencies with a qualified staff.

Some of us are frightened of psychotherapy because of a thought that we may find out we are 'really bad' people. Although this is a common fear associated with psychotherapy, it has no basis. We have this fear because we have never had a true sense of who we are, and we do not fully appreciate ourselves.

Take the risk. We will discover there is nothing 'bad' about us. Like everyone else, there will be aspects about ourselves we may not like. Only when we know these aspects can we modify and integrate them.

> **Psychotherapy means more than just looking at the problems and difficulties of childhood. It is not so much a process of who is to blame, as a process of understanding causes and effects. It looks at how we, as children, responded in certain situations. These responses created our defenses, motivations and patterns of behavior that we unconsciously carried into adulthood, but which may not be appropriate now. When we become aware of these responses, we are then able to change them if we want to.**

Relaxation

In an effort to help us relax, many of us are prescribed tranquilizers. However, this does not teach us management skills. While we need to be able to control our disorder, our need to be in control prevents us from relaxing. Relaxing means letting go of this dysfunctional control. In letting go, we gain a much healthier way of control.

Relaxation doesn't mean curling up with a book or watching television. If it were that simple, we wouldn't have the disorder in the first place. Establishing the discipline of practicing a relaxation technique may appear inconvenient to some people, despite the extraordinary inconvenience of their disorder, but recovery is worth the effort.

The main relaxation techniques are various forms of progressive muscle relaxation, and meditation. Progressive muscle relaxation is a step-by-step technique which teaches us to tense, then relax the major muscle groups in our bodies. If practiced successfully, our minds also begin to relax. As our minds relax we may find ourselves meditating.

Meditation techniques work in the opposite way. If our practice is successful our minds relax first, then our bodies relax easily and effortlessly by themselves.

Meditation is over five thousand years old and while we use meditation as a relaxation technique, it is also the oldest cognitive technique in the world. Besides enabling us to access deep levels of relaxation, meditation teaches us how to be aware of and control our thoughts.

Chapter seven will outline two meditation techniques. I used meditation because I found it was simpler and easier for me, during the years I had panic disorder/agoraphobia. This is also true for many people I have worked with over the years. This doesn't mean progressive muscle relaxation doesn't work—it does, and I have known people who find it easier. It is an individual choice.

- **Much of our recovery depends on our commitment to lower and keep down our levels of anxiety and panic. Practicing a relaxation technique is a proven natural way to do this.**

An overview

When we look at the list of therapies it can be quite overwhelming. It isn't really as daunting as it looks. Understanding of the disorders has now come a long way and freedom from the disorders is a reality for many of us. Treatment programs which incorporate relaxation, breathing techniques and cognitive behavioral therapy have been 'associated with dramatic success' (Otto et al. 1994). A program, conducted in Queensland which uses similar methods has shown 'long term improvements', which is not only beneficial for people with the disorder as it 'quickly restores functioning', but is also 'cost effective' (Evans 1995), an important issue in any treatment service which cannot be ignored.

Recovery is a step-by-step process. While cognitive behavioral skills are the most important, short-term medication may be required; conversely if drug or alcohol dependence is involved, this will also need to be worked with. After your cognitive skills are sufficiently developed and your life is coming back on track you may want to address any outstanding personal issues by seeing a skilled psychotherapist. The secret is to use the various therapies we need when we need them. Combined together we can take the power back.

Part 2

Five Steps to Freedom

Chapter 5

Steps 1 and 2
Understanding
—Acceptance

The development of the disorders can destroy our lives. We can live with the power of the disorder for many years and no matter what we do, we feel completely powerless.

Recovery for many of us who have had panic disorder means we still can experience an occasional attack. The difference between panic disorder and recovery means we have taken the power back and are no longer afraid of the attack or anxiety. We have shifted the power balance. There are no more 'what ifs', but instead we have developed an attitude of 'so what', irrespective of how violent the occasional attack may feel. 'So what', means we have taken back the power.

Compassion

A major obstacle to taking back the power is the lack of compassion we have for ourselves. Compassion in this instance is the acknowledgement, and the capacity to fully feel the pain of our own suffering without mentally abusing ourselves, 'I am hopeless, stupid, worthless etc' and without the brutal self-hatred many of us feel.

In the early stages of the disorders many of us say, 'This is not me, I am not like this', and in doing so we negate and invalidate our own suffering and pain. Most of us cannot see, let alone acknowledge or appreciate our own strength and courage, which has bought us thus far. Taking back the power means learning to be compassionate toward ourselves. Only then can we begin to take back the power from the disorders.

Compassion for ourselves, combined with understanding is the first step. It is important we understand what is happening to us and why it is happening. When we understand and accept that understanding, we can begin to work towards recovery.

Stress

Everyone experiences stress, and everyone reacts in different ways when they reach their individual threshold to stress. For example, some people will experience high blood pressure, others may develop an ulcer. When we reach the limit of our threshold to stress we experience a panic attack. Our lack of understanding and our reactions of fear and anxiety place us under further stress, and the vicious circle begins. Recovery does not necessarily mean the end of attacks. However, it does mean the end of fear, panic, anxiety and the secondary conditions.

· **Anxiety disorders are not life-threatening in themselves. It is**
· **only our lack of understanding which makes them appear so.**

Panic attacks

A panic attack, either spontaneous, cued or situationally predisposed; is diagnosed when we experience four or more of the symptoms described in chapter two. However, a large group of us also experience other sensations as the attack, and we panic as a result (Arthur-Jones et al 1994).

Notice the separation of the words 'panic' and 'attack'. Many of us experience an attack and then react with fear and panic. Learning to see this separation is an important step in recovery.

Some people will dissociate first, and panic at the sensations of dissociation. Other people describe their attack as being like an electric shock, or an intense burning, tingling sensation moving through the body. Some report that it feels like a wave of unusual energy surging through them. The attack itself is usually experienced as beginning in the feet, surging through the body, over the head and back down through the body again (Arthur-Jones 1994). Or it is likened to a white-hot flame, starting 'just below the breast bone, passing through the chest, up the spine, into the face, down the arms and even down to the groin and to the tips of the toes' (Weekes 1992).

These sensations can occur at anytime during the day or night. They have been described in sleep research literature since 1890 and are said to occur during the hypnagogic first stage of sleep and/or during the transition from REM sleep to the deeper stage of sleep. Sleep researchers describe it as an 'upward surge of indescribable nature, an electric sort of feeling ascending from the abdomen to the head, sometimes followed by bodily jerks or a violent explosion and/or a flash of light'. The researchers also note that 'a sense of alarm follows the experience' (Oswald 1962).

For the sake of brevity I call all the above experiences 'surge' attacks. Throughout the rest of the book I will refer to all panic attacks as 'attacks'. When I am describing particular attacks, I will refer to them by their individual 'name'.

As the 'surge' goes through our body, our heart and respiration rates increase, we may feel nauseated, we may feel dizzy as if we are going to faint, we may shake or tremble, we may feel hot or cold flushes, and may dissociate. The attack is extremely powerful and most of us feel as if we are going to die, so it is completely natural and normal to become frightened and panic. Recovery means we may occasionally experience these sensations, but instead of reacting with fear and panic, we now just let them happen. As I have said, we need to develop an attitude towards them of 'so what' instead of 'what if'. I will discuss this further in chapter eight.

The first steps toward recovery

If you haven't been diagnosed as having panic attacks or panic-related anxiety disorder, but think this may be what you are experiencing, speak to a doctor. Don't self-diagnose. You need to know exactly what it is you are trying to recover from.

The attacks are not harmful, despite the multitude of sensations and symptoms we all experience. We can take back the power by learning to minimize their impact through understanding and accepting how the attacks and the anxiety are being perpetuated.

Understanding is the first step in taking back the power and in working toward recovery.

> **Recovery is a step-by-step process. If we have been diagnosed as having a panic-related anxiety disorder, the first step is to fully understand the disorder and to accept the diagnosis.**

The fight-and-flight response

When we experience an attack or anxiety, we react with fear. It is our reaction of fear that keeps us trapped. Our feelings of fear continually activate the fight-and-flight response.

The fight-and-flight response is an automatic response by our bodies when we perceive ourselves to be in danger. Stress hormones, including adrenalin, are released into our bloodstream to prepare us either to flee the situation or to stay and confront it. Our heart rate increases, our breathing becomes rapid and shallow, we may shake or tremble or perspire profusely. The effects of the adrenalin combine with those of the attack, and heighten the severity of the attack.

Although the attack is self-limiting and does subside, our perception that it is life-threatening makes us feel as if we are in constant danger. The threat of danger automatically activates the fight-and-flight response.

As many of us become continually frightened and anxious we constantly experience the effects of adrenalin in the bloodstream. We interpret the effects as being something other than what they really are, so we become more frightened and more trapped in the vicious circle. The more frightened and anxious we are, the more adrenalin is released. The more adrenalin, the more the effects increase.

Although there is a lack of understanding about anxiety disorders by the health professions, they do understand the fight-and-flight response. They know and understand the body's response to a feeling of fear is fight-and-flight. They also know once we lose our fear the fight-and-flight response will stop. Losing the fear of what is happening to us is one of the major factors in our long-term recovery. Initially it is difficult because we do not have the overall understanding to help us lose the fear. We need to understand why we are not going to die, go insane or lose control through our anxiety disorder.

Fear of death

Heart symptoms

The most common fear we have is that we will die from a heart attack. Besides having a rapid heartbeat, some people experience palpitations or 'missed' heartbeats. They are not dangerous, and will not hurt us in any way. The more we fear them, the more adrenalin is released, so the cycle continues.

Muscle tension

The fear of having a heart attack is compounded by the tightness or pain which may be experienced in the chest, arms and jaw. It can also be felt in our neck and throat. It doesn't mean there is anything seriously wrong. Stress and tension cause our muscles to tighten. The tension will disappear once we have begun to let go of the fear and anxiety.

Throat constriction

Another symptom which causes a great deal of fear is the feeling of tightness or constriction in the throat, as it feels as if the air supply will be cut off. It won't. The tightness is a sign of just how tense we are. When we reduce the tension this symptom will disappear.

Breathing difficulties

The rapid and shallow breathing caused by the release of adrenalin may lead to over-breathing. Some people become so frightened of their shallow breathing they feel as if their breathing will stop completely. In other instances people feel they can't take a deep breath because of the tightness in their chest.

Over-breathing is known as hyperventilation, and its symptoms are similar to those of an attack. We can experience pins and needles, light-headedness and dizziness. When we hyperventilate the original symptoms of the attack are intensified by the additional symptoms of hyperventilation.

I have only met a few people who have actually fainted. Some people have told me they have occasionally fallen to the floor, but even then they have never lost consciousness. Even if it does happen, there is nothing to be alarmed about. It is just the body's way of getting control of the situation so it can stabilize itself.

It is important to point out that if this hasn't already happened, then it probably never will. If it were going to happen it would have during the initial stages of the disorder.

The effects of hyperventilation can be alleviated quite easily by taking the time to breathe very slowly and deeply. Sometimes just holding our breath for ten seconds can help to return breathing to normal.

Another simple and effective way to stop these symptoms is to cup our hands over our mouth and nose and breathe into them. We will feel the symptoms easing. This method is a variation on the most common technique of easing hyper-ventilation—breathing into a paper bag. However, most of us do not want to do that, because we do not want to draw attention to ourselves.

With so many symptoms centered on our heart and breathing it is only natural we are frightened we may die. Understanding why we have these symptoms, and understanding why they won't hurt us, will help us to lose the fear. When we lose the fear we turn off the adrenalin and the symptoms ease.

> **When we are assured by our doctor that there is nothing wrong with our heart and our breathing, we need to accept it. Our recovery depends upon it. If we don't accept it, we will continue to be afraid of our experiences and our fear will perpetuate the disorder. If we still doubt the diagnosis or experience any new symptoms, then we need to speak to our doctor again.**

Fear of insanity

The fear of insanity is the second most common fear. We all try to get control over what is happening to us and the harder we fight, the worse we get.

Trying to understand what is happening to us continually pushes us to the limits of our knowledge. We cannot find anything in our past experience that even comes close to what we are experiencing now, so many of us feel we are going insane.

We're not, although it often feels like it. Some of the other symptoms we experience don't help to break this fear; they usually add to it.

Dissociation

As I have discussed in chapter two, the role dissociation plays in anxiety disorders is now being examined. From what I have found over the years, the ability to dissociate is found in a large subgroup of people who experience spontaneous panic attacks. Dissociation can also be described as altered or discrete states of consciousness or trance states. Altered or trance states are found in many cultures. They can be an 'accepted expression of cultural or religious experience in many societies' (APA 1994). A leading expert in altered or discrete states, Dr Charles Tart (1972) comments that many other cultures, 'believe that almost every normal adult has the ability to go into a trance state'.

These states are simply mental states where the focus is not fixed in normal every-day attentiveness but is allowed to drift or move more inwardly. Attention can fall into reverie, or visualization, or even emptiness. In some cultures and societies, trance states are used deliberately to develop intuition or attain healing or spiritual goals.

Individuals in these societies induce trance states not only by meditation, but by fasting, sleep deprivation and other forms of physiological stress. For those of us who have the ability to dissociate, major stress can make us more vulnerable to dissociation, or the stress can be a cause of our not eating properly or of losing sleep, which in turn increases our vulnerability to dissociate.

The ability to dissociate is not harmful in itself, but our lack of understanding of the phenomena can lead to acute anxiety and panic. Although some people with panic disorder report they are not frightened of these sensations, others are, and the fear contributes to the feeling of going insane or loss of control.

It has been assumed that dissociation is an effect of a panic attack and some people use these states as a form of 'escape' from the anxiety or the attack. While I have seen this in some cases, other people are aware it is the dissociation which triggers the panic (Arthur-Jones 1994).

People who do dissociate 'may display high hypnotizability and high dissociative capacity' (APA 1994). It may be this 'high hypnotizability' in some of us which triggers the spontaneous attacks.

Inducing dissociative states when we are vulnerable to them is incredibly easy. Over the years I have noticed the extent to which many of us stare. At the walls, at the computer, at the TV screen, at a book and also when we are driving. We stare at a red light, at the car in front of us, at the road ahead. When we are vulnerable we can induce a trance state very quickly and without our realising it. Without warning, we can feel the various sensations of dissociation.

In the eastern traditions, open-eyed meditation is an advanced meditation technique, usually only taught to skilled practitioners (Brunton 1965). Yet many of us are unconsciously practising a similar method of 'meditation'. In many cases we do induce a dissociative state and panic as the result.

Our self absorption can be absolute, and this self absorption is similar to other meditation techniques. We need to be aware that our self absorption can be significant enough to also induce dissociative states. Some people also report fluorescent lighting can also induce these states (Arthur-Jones 1994).

Dissociation can also occur when we begin to relax. In contradiction to the prevailing thought that when we relax we have more time to think about our symptoms, many of us actually dissociate as we relax and then become anxious and/or panic.

One such research paper, which links dizziness to depersonalisation, theorizes that it is not so much what we are doing at the time we dissociate, 'it is the magnitude of the change [of consciousness]...which is significant' (Fewtrell et al 1988).

I, and other people who dissociate, have noticed some shifts of consciousness are accompanied by the 'surge attacks'; along with a rapid beating heart; difficulty in breathing and dizziness. When we lose our fear of the dissociated state and the 'surge' sensations our heart rate and breathing can return to normal in a matter of seconds.

It is interesting to note, nocturnal panic attacks occur, as I have said, during the transition from stage two to stage three sleep. In other words, during a change in consciousness.

Our fear of the dissociated states will not only hold us in them, it will induce further symptoms. To end the dissociated state all we need to is to break our stare, blink our eyes and/or pull back from our deep self absorption. If we wake in a dissociated state it is simply a matter of being aware we are dissociating and giving ourselves a minute or so to let our consciousness return to its waking state. Or if it wakes us in the middle of the night, we can just be aware we are dissociating and go back to sleep.

Fear of losing control

This is the third most common fear. Our lack of understanding of the disorder accentuates this fear. We feel so much has already happened which we haven't been able to control, and every day seems to bring with it new symptoms and new fears. We can't help but feel the time will come when we will lose control completely. People fear they will faint, have an attack of diarrhea, lose control of their bladder, be sick or literally lose control. Most of these symptoms are a result of the fight and flight response. The more we fear them, the more we turn on the adrenalin. Losing our fear of them turns it off. I will discuss how to in chapter eight.

Feeling faint

The sensation of feeling faint and/or dizzy can be a result of either not eating, depersonalization or hyperventilation, or a combination of all three! The nausea many people feel can result in them not eating. Not just occasionally missing meals, but simply not eating. This is turn will cause feelings of faintness or dizziness, shaking and an overall sense of weakness.

We forget these sensations are a natural result of not eating and put them down to the anxiety, which in turn adds to the cycle. If we don't eat we can become more vulnerable to dissociation. Attention to diet is extremely important. If you are experiencing difficulty in being able to eat, it is important that you speak with your doctor.

If dizziness or feeling faint is a result of dissociation, we can break the dissociated state, or if it is a result of hyperventilation we can adjust our breathing.

Loss of control over body

We can feel as if we may lose control of our bowel or bladder, or that we will be sick. Nausea can become our constant companion, and if we look at all our symptoms it is no wonder. Our body does feel as if it is out of control.

When we imagine these events happening, we also imagine our embarrassment and humiliation. Naturally, this only increases the fear.

Again, I rarely meet anyone who has had these fears realized, although people speak of their 'close calls'. When we learn panic anxiety management skills, we can take back the power over the fear and anxiety and turn off the fight and flight response.

Literally losing control

This fear can be terrifying. People interpret it to mean they may act uncontrollably and hurt themselves or others. They don't.

The fear of losing control completely comes from the loss of control we have already experienced. The harder we fight to get control, the more we lose control. Not over ourselves, but over our life.

I have never heard of anyone losing complete control over themselves. Again, if this was going to happen it would have happened with the first attack. It will not happen in the future. Recovery means letting go of the control we are fighting so hard to maintain. Letting go of this control means we gain control. Being in control means we will lose the fear of losing control completely.

Acceptance

Understanding our disorder is the first step in taking the power back. Acceptance is the second step. When we have been diagnosed as having an anxiety disorder we need to accept it, otherwise we will not be able to recover.

The starting point is to accept: 'This is me and I have an anxiety disorder'. We need to totally accept the disorder and ourselves, not with fear and not with shame or humiliation, but with understanding and compassion. When we can fully accept ourselves as we are at the moment, we can begin to work towards the future when we won't have an anxiety disorder.

Even when we have accepted the anxiety disorder it can still dominate our life. Through our fear we remain passive. If we feel angry or frustrated we take it out on ourselves. Why? Why aren't we angry at the disorder? It is destroying our lives. We need to take the power back. We need to dominate it. Everyone wants to recover, but we need to reach a point where enough is enough. The power of our anger and frustration can motivate us in developing an attitude of, 'I will recover no matter what!'

'No matter what' means our recovery is number one priority. We become disciplined in our approach to meditation or relaxation and our other management strategies.

As our power and confidence develop, 'no matter what' means we challenge our thoughts. We challenge our fear. We challenge the anxiety and our attacks. How dare they do this to us?

Have you ever tried to have an attack? Have you ever tried to be anxious? Try. See what happens.

As I mentioned in chapter four, our anger can be the 'rocketship' to recovery. We can use our anger and frustration against the disorder, instead of against ourselves. Our anger and frustration can help break its dominance. Our anger at this level of acceptance is stronger than our fear. We take back the power. The dominance of the disorder is broken permanently.

The disorders do feel as if they push us to our limits, physically, mentally, emotionally and in some cases spiritually. We survive—but we can do more than just survive, we can recover. We can take back the power.

Chapter 6

Step 3
Meditation:
Why?

Why meditation?

As I have been discussing throughout the book, our recovery depends upon learning to manage our anxiety and attacks ourselves. Understanding and accepting our disorder are the first two steps to taking the power back. Learning to manage the attacks and anxiety are the third and fourth step.

This chapter will look at meditation; what it is and why it works. In the next chapter two different meditation techniques will be described.

Managing them means we need to follow a disciplined approach to a formal relaxation program. At first glance some people hesitate. Although they want to recover they don't like the idea of having to become disciplined in their approach to relaxation.

Meditation can become a superior relaxation technique if it is practiced daily. In one way, 'having to relax' is a contradiction to the practice itself, but many of us find we reach the stage where we do it because we want to, not because we have to.

Meditation has been the subject of research since the late 1960s and is now being used in many treatments in conjunction with conventional medical practices. It is being used to improve the quality of life for people who have cancer, AIDS or high blood pressure, and to help people who have an addiction to narcotics. Meditation also reduces anxiety levels in anxiety disorders. One study showed 'significant reductions in anxiety and depression' and that it is effective in panic disorder with or without agoraphobia and generalized anxiety disorder (Kabat-Zinn 1992).

If we have the ability to dissociate, we will find meditation quite easy, because we are already accessing various states of consciousness. We can use meditation as an 'exposure' technique to become more familiar with altered states. The more familiar we become with them, the more we will lose our fear of them.

> Our recovery depends upon our ability to bring down and keep down our anxiety level. Recovery means having to change some of our previous ways of dealing with certain aspects of our life. Becoming disciplined in a relaxation technique is an important step in our overall commitment to recovery.

The background of meditation

Meditation is an integral part of Eastern religions and forms the basis of some Christian traditions. This gives rise to the many myths surrounding meditation. As a consequence some people are unsure of meditation and are concerned about practising it. Therefore it is important for these issues to be discussed. If we have doubts about meditation because of our religious background, we need to speak to our minister or priest and be guided by our own feelings of what is right for us.

Meditation is like so many of the other Eastern techniques and disciplines we have adopted, such as various martial arts, tai chi and yoga. In India the word 'yoga' is a generic name for a multitude of meditation disciplines. The word 'yoga' was originally defined as 'the way to go', but more recently it has been defined simply as 'union'.

We associate yoga with the practice of gentle physical and breathing exercises. This form of yoga is derived from a very strict meditation discipline called 'hatha yoga'. The West has adapted hatha yoga to its needs by stripping it of all its religious and ascetic practices. This form of yoga is now an accepted part of our Western lifestyle.

Other forms of meditation from the Eastern traditions have also been adapted. The comprehensive and intricate visualisations of various deities have been replaced with images of beaches or forests, the devotional 'gazing' has been replaced with flowers or candles, and the sacred mantras have been replaced with everyday words.

There is nothing mysterious in these techniques. The strict adherence and disciplines required for their religious and philosophical aspects have been stripped away, leaving their bare essence, techniques for relaxation and quieting the mind. Learning to meditate does not mean we have to change our religion, our lifestyle or our diet. The only thing which will change will be our response to stress and anxiety.

Misconceptions

There are other misconceptions which people have about meditation. Some people see meditation as an escape from reality or a selfish preoccupation. It is neither. A normal meditation time is twenty minutes, twice a day. This hardly constitutes an escape from reality, nor can it be regarded as selfish. Everyone needs to have time to themselves. It is not selfish to want time alone, it is natural and normal. Meditation will improve your capacity to be present in the world.

The disorder and agoraphobia mean we cannot contribute as much as we would like to our daily family situation. Practising meditation can mean a major step for our overall recovery. Recovery means we can contribute more, not only to the family but also to ourselves. Wanting to take time out, to help the recovery process, should never be considered selfish.

Taking the time to stop and meditate can be a problem for some people. Meditation is usually practiced for two twenty-minute periods each day, although a number of people meditate for only one twenty-minute period each day and still find it beneficial. Other people tell themselves they can spare no time for meditation at all, despite the fact that the disorder may consume them twenty-four hours a day. It is a matter of making a choice in our priorities. It can mean the difference between ongoing anxiety, and our recovery.

Another myth about meditation is the idea that, when meditating, we may be leaving ourselves exposed to other influences. This does not and cannot happen. Even in the deepest phase of meditation we are always in complete control of ourselves. We are always aware of everything within and outside ourselves. When we are asleep we are not consciously aware of anything, yet we will wake up should there be any internal or external threat. In meditation we don't need to 'become' aware because we are consciously aware, and consciously in control, the whole time.

The relaxation response

In his book *The Relaxation Response* (1975), Dr Herbert Benson discusses the meditative state, which he calls the relaxation response, and makes a comparison between the relaxation response and the fight-and-flight response, suggesting that they are complete opposites. Both responses are controlled by an area of the brain called the *hypothalamus*. As the fight-and-flight response is a natural response which happens automatically in time of danger, Dr Benson suggests the relaxation response—the meditative response—is also a natural response, which happens as we begin to relax.

The fight-and-flight response causes much of our ongoing distress. The relaxation response, being its direct opposite, can help to ease this distress.

Learning to let go

In meditation, as in any relaxation technique, the first requirement is to let the relaxation process happen. It means not only letting go of our thoughts, feelings and emotions, but letting go of our control. As I have already discussed in chapter three, our need to be in control of ourselves and our environment is one of the major factors in the perpetuation of the disorder. Letting go of this control is essential to recovery.

> **Some of us find the prospect of letting go in meditation quite fearful. It can be too frightening even to think about it. We may think that by letting go we will lose control, and all our worst fears will come true. This is not the case. By letting go we are actually gaining control, not losing it.**

Sometimes we may experience a 'surge' attack during meditation. If this or other types of attacks happen in meditation, the secret is to let them happen. Not to fight them, but let them come. We keep our mind focused on our meditation technique. Although this may seem frightening as you read this, in actuality it isn't frightening. When you let the attack happen and keep focused on your meditation, the attack will move through your body and disappear as quickly as it came. This is taking back the power.

Some meditators experience energy sensations or changes in their breathing as they develop their sitting practices. These are harmless signs of internal shifts in consciousness and are generally considered signs of progress, which will pass if they are simply observed.

It may take some time for people to gain the confidence to begin to let go of their control. Other people are able to let go within meditation immediately, and as they let go they can meditate naturally and easily. This is the beginning of full recovery. It is a very important step, because meditation teaches us that it is all right to let go of the control we are trying so hard to maintain. As we let go of this control we realize our major fears don't come true, and as our practice continues over time we begin to understand why they never will.

Learning about ourselves

Another positive aspect of the dynamics of meditation is that it can teach us even more about ourselves. Over a period of time and with continued practice, meditation begins to work on many subtle levels. The quiet of meditation gives us the chance to integrate many aspects of ourselves. This happens subconsciously and we don't become aware of this process straight away. Slowly and subtly the integration breaks through into our consciousness. We begin to see changes in how we perceive and react to the various day-to-day situations which arise.

A helpful analogy is using the 'sort' command on a database. The database contains a lot of data which needs be sorted into alphabetical order. The computer operator presses the 'sort' key, and the computer sorts and rearranges the information into strict alphabetical order.

Meditation works something like this. It helps to process all the information we are holding in our 'database'. It begins to sort everything into a more ordered view. Sometimes the process of meditation will 'throw out a file' for us to look at, other times it gets on with what it has to do without any reference to us. Just like a computer! The result is a changed and more ordered perception of ourselves and our environment.

This is part of the reason why meditation and psychotherapy 'complement' one another. One study of meditation states that 'meditation may facilitate the psychotherapeutic process' (Task Force on Meditation, 1977).

The release of stress

Each meditation session should be for twenty minutes. In the case of meditation, more is not necessarily better. Within the twenty minutes, accumulated stress and emotions are being released. It is better if this release is done slowly and gradually. If our meditation time is extended, it is possible that feelings such as grief, sadness or anger, of which we were unaware, may arise. As I said, it will sometimes 'throw out a file' for us to look at.

On rare occasions this may happen during the twenty-minute sessions. If it does and if we feel distressed, we can reduce the meditation time to ten minutes, gradually building back up to twenty minutes. It is better to cut down the length of meditation time than to stop meditating altogether.

After twelve or eighteen months of regular meditation, session times can be slowly extended up to an hour. The releasing process is an ongoing one, but with experience people are able to understand and not become hesitant if they experience a release of feelings or emotions. Many people actually cultivate such releases because they see how beneficial they are in the long term.

The daily practice of meditation does require discipline, but we shouldn't feel guilty if we miss a meditation session. Missing one or two sessions happens to everyone. Only after days or weeks without meditating should we seriously question our motivation—or lack of it.

Guide to successful meditation

While the meditation process produces a feeling of quiet, don't expect it to happen. Just let the meditation process happen naturally and easily. If we expect it to happen, it doesn't. If we expect it to happen we spend the whole meditation session not meditating, but looking for the quiet and wondering when it will happen. When we are meditating correctly our meditation will lead us effortlessly and naturally to the full meditative state. Don't fight thoughts, feelings or emotions. Let them come and let them go. Don't become involved with them by hooking into them. Meditation is not a process of trying to eliminate all thoughts or feelings. Nor is it a process of trying to think of nothing, which is a contradiction in itself. The 'no-thinking' will happen naturally as we move into the deeper stages. The rising and falling of our thoughts are part of the whole process. They will slow down and finally cease naturally as we enter the full meditative state.

- As the meditation process unfolds, some people become anxious when they notice their breathing slowing down. Sometimes it feels as if you are hardly breathing at all. This can be disconcerting at first, especially for people who have this fear. There is nothing to worry about. The slowing down of our breathing indicates we are beginning to relax deeply. It is a positive sign that the meditation session is going well.
- If you are using a word or mantra technique to meditate don't worry when the technique becomes distorted or disappears altogether in the course of your meditation. This is another indication of successful meditation.
- Some people find they go to sleep during meditation. Although most meditation teachers advise their students to remain alert and not go to sleep, I feel somewhat differently about it in the case of anxiety disorders. Firstly, it is a good sign that the practice is going well. If we can let go and relax enough to sleep, then in the beginning this is all that matters. In this instance, meditation is being used as a relaxation technique. Many people with the disorder have difficulty in sleeping. If meditation means people are able to catch up on sleep, then the practice is successful. Most people who do go to sleep during meditation find they do so for about forty-five minutes, and on awakening they feel the benefits. Take it as it comes. In time we all reach the stage when we actually meditate instead of going to sleep.
- Don't set an alarm clock to time your meditation. There is nothing worse than being brought out of meditation by a loud noise. It is quite easy to time your meditation. Most of us place a watch in a convenient position and during the meditation will open our eyes to check the time. After a few days most of us are able to gauge when the twenty minutes are over without needing to check.

Sometimes the twenty minutes are over so quickly we wonder if our watches are working correctly; on other occasions the time seems to go very slowly and we become irritated. If this happens, it may be beneficial to end the meditation session and try again later.

61

When the meditation session is over, we sit quietly with our eyes closed for a couple of minutes before getting up. This allows us to re-orient ourselves gently and naturally. There may be times when we will need to break our meditation session for one reason or another. If this happens, try to return to it as soon as possible to finish the remaining time.

- Outside noises may interfere. Acknowledge that they are happening, but don't become caught up in them. Let them happen and let go of the irritated thoughts.

- Avoid drinking coffee and other products with caffeine in them before meditation. Caffeine is a stimulant. Meditation is for relaxation. It is also a good idea not to meditate just after eating, because our digestive systems slow down during meditation.

- Initially, each meditation session will be different from the previous one. Some will be great, others not so good. Remember that learning to meditate is learning a new skill. For the first twelve months most people find each of their meditation sessions are different. It is this difference between sessions which teaches us more about the whole process.

- It is important to go with whatever happens. Don't stifle a cough or yawn or sneeze. Do whatever feels necessary and is comfortable.

Chapter 7

Step 3
Meditation:
How?

Two meditation techniques

The word technique

The first meditation technique I will discuss is derived from a yoga discipline called mantra yoga. While hatha yoga uses breathing and physical exercise to enter the meditative state, mantra yoga uses a mantra—a sound or a devotional word or phrase which we silently repeat to ourselves. 'Om', which is spelt 'aum', is a mantra most of us have heard of.

The Western adaptation of mantra yoga uses a word instead of the traditional mantra. This meditation technique involves the silent repetition of a word to focus our minds on. This technique is not used in conjunction with a breathing technique. All it involves is the repetition of a word.

Choosing a word

What word to use is a matter of individual choice. As a general guide, make sure the word is short. Some people use 'still' or 'hush' or, depending upon the person's religious background, they may choose a word which has a deeper meaning for them. Dr Benson (1975) in *The Relaxation Response* uses the word 'one'. Other people use nonsensical words which have no meaning at all.

Choosing a mantra

There is no harm in deciding to use a mantra. 'Aum' is the best-known mantra and has been translated as meaning 'the sound of the universe'. Two other well known mantras are 'sharma', which has been translated as meaning 'quietude' or 'shantih', meaning 'peace' or 'calm'.

I have found it better to stay away from English words such as 'peace' or 'calm'. We have so many negative associations with these words: 'Calm down', 'Why can't I get any peace?' that we may have difficulty in meditating.

The word, or mantra, is used as a focal point during the meditation. As our practice continues we become conditioned to our word or mantra, and over time the word or mantra becomes associated with the deeper levels of meditation. This makes our practice of meditation easier, because the word or mantra will take us directly to the deeper levels of meditation without us having to go through the preliminary stages.

This is why it is better not to continually change the word or mantra. Changing it can lead to frustration with the whole process. We need to become relaxed, not frustrated.

The only exception to this is when a word, mantra or even an image comes spontaneously during the meditation session. If this happens, then use that word, mantra or image. Meditation teaches us in sometimes very subtle ways. It helps us get in touch with our real selves. The spontaneous rising of a word, mantra or image is part of this.

Confusion

People occasionally become confused in their choice of word. They can spend many meditation sessions experimenting with one word or another, and consequently do not achieve any results whatsoever. In such cases it is a good idea to use a breathing technique instead.

Breathing techniques

The breathing techniques I will discuss are based on the Buddhist mindfulness meditation, which focuses, not on a word or mantra, but on the breath. This can be frightening for some people because of their inability to take a deep breath. While this technique does not involve deep breathing, it may be more advisable for these people to use the word technique instead.

There are two ways the breathing technique can be used. The first is being 'mindful' of our breathing—watching the breathing process, watching the rise and fall of our breath, as we inhale and exhale. The act of watching the breath becomes the focus. Simple!

The second way is to count each breath. Counting each breath becomes the technique. As we begin to meditate, the first breath we take is counted as 'one', the second 'two' and so on until breath number five. After breath number five the count begins again at 'one', and so on.

Sometimes people use both a word and the first breathing technique. This will not cause any problems and if it feels right, then use them both. At this stage, however, remember it is better to decide on which technique to use and then stay with it.

Many people find having a piece of meditation or classical music playing in the background quite beneficial as it helps to block out any distracting sounds and helps them to let go more easily.

It is best not to use the word, mantra or breathing technique during our normal daily life when we are anxious or having an attack. As our technique becomes linked to the meditative state, the last thing we need is to find we have begun to associate it with anxiety and attacks. Some people have a 'stand by' word or phrase they use in times of great distress, which they find can be quite beneficial. They leave their main word or mantra for their regular practice of meditation.

The practice of meditation

Sit comfortably in a chair and close your eyes. After a few seconds begin to lightly concentrate on either the silent repetition of your word or the breathing technique. There is no need for intense concentration. Just be aware as you silently repeat your word or focus on your breathing. Thoughts will intrude. In the early stages it is very easy to get caught up in the thoughts. Become aware that your technique has been lost and has been replaced by thoughts. Gently let the thoughts go, by ceasing to think of them or about them, and return your awareness to the technique of meditation.

It is important not to worry about the thoughts which break through. This is the one basic mistake most of us make in meditation. When we first learn to meditate we constantly get caught up in our thoughts. We need to learn to be aware, let them go and return to our meditation technique. As our skill develops, our minds become more disciplined and settle much more easily.

The process of meditation can be summarised as follows:

1   As we begin the practice of meditation we bring our attention to the technique we have chosen, either by silently repeating a word or mantra, or by focusing on our breathing.
2   The meditation practice is lost as we become caught up in our thoughts.
3   We become aware we have lost our practice.
4   We let go of our thoughts and we ...
1   Return back to our practice.
2   Again we become caught up in our thoughts and we lose our practice.
3   We again become aware we have lost our practice.
4   We let go of our thoughts and we ...
1   Return our attention back to our practice.

This is the process of meditation. These are the four stages everyone works through. This is also the first stage of learning to develop control over our thoughts. It is no wonder the Eastern traditions refer to 'the monkey mind'. As we learn to meditate we begin to see how much our thoughts run and jump all over the place!

There are two ways people experience the preliminary stages of meditation. Some people will be able to focus their attention on their chosen technique, and that is all they need to do to free their minds from any other thought. Their attention will be broken as a thought rises into consciousness. The thought then becomes the focus of attention and their technique will disappear completely. When they become aware and bring their attention back to the technique their thoughts will disappear.

Other people will be aware of the repetition of their technique and the rising and falling of thoughts at the same time. The rise and fall of their thoughts may be in the 'background' while their attention is focused on their technique in the 'foreground', or vice versa. When they become aware that their attention is on their thoughts, they let them go and the thoughts drift into the background again.

CASE HISTORIES

Sandra

It was Sandra's first meditation lesson. She was feeling apprehensive. She glanced around the room and wondered if other people were feeling the same way. She closed her eyes and began to practise the meditation technique she had chosen. At first she felt self-conscious and wanted to laugh out loud. She couldn't understand how this would help her with her anxiety and attacks. Gradually Sandra became aware of a gentle heaviness slowly moving through her body. A wave of fear went through her, but she allowed it to pass without resisting it. She felt herself drifting into deeper and deeper levels of relaxation. The voice of Sandra's instructor, ending the meditation session, broke into the silent depths of her meditation. Slowly Sandra opened her eyes. She had done it! She was able to meditate.

Philip

Deciding to find time to meditate can be a problem for many people, of whom Philip was one. Philip had been practising meditation on and off for several months. He had become aware that he always had a bad day if he didn't meditate the night before, but wished there was an easier way to control his anxiety. He 'didn't have time' and it was such an effort to try to make time. He felt he would just have to put up with the anxiety until a 'real' cure was found.

Joanne

Some people experience symptoms similar to those of panic attacks in meditation. Joanne did, while she was in the deeper stages of meditation. Instead of reacting with fear, Joanne was able to let them happen and they went as quickly as they came. This gave Joanne the courage to let them happen during the day, when she wasn't meditating. Again, they went as quickly as they came. Joanne had found the key to her recovery.

Stages of meditation

There are various phases of the meditative process. Most people experience them in varying degrees. Some people become very worried about these experiences. Therefore it is important to discuss them.

The one experience people worry about is the sensation of their body relaxing. Sometimes people have been so tense for so many years they have forgotten what it is like to feel even slightly relaxed. As their bodies begin to let go of the tension, people become anxious and interpret the sensations as a sign that their worst fears are about to come true. They don't.

The first stage of meditation can be difficult for beginners. Our thoughts are not used to being ignored and they continually break through and demand attention. As long as we can accept this as normal and let go of them without becoming frustrated, we can move into the second stage of meditation.

As we enter the second stage of meditation we feel the quiet settle over us. Our breathing begins to slow down. Our thoughts are still rising and falling, but our attention is now much more focused on our technique. Everything moves into the background as our quietness grows.

We enter the third stage. Our breathing slows down even further and our body becomes deeply relaxed. We may feel as if we are as light as a feather, or we may feel a comfortable heaviness. We become aware that the continuous stream of thoughts has broken. They now rise slowly and separate from each other. Individually, they quietly rise and fall without us becoming distracted by them. We find our word or mantra becomes distorted. This is what is supposed to happen. Some of us may see brilliant white, black or other swirls of colour. We can use them to take ourselves deeper. Our thoughts drift in and out, slowly and quietly.

We then enter the full meditative state in which there is perfect quietness, an absence of thought, feeling or emotions. Unlike the stages of deep sleep, this state of consciousness is very dynamic. There is full awareness of 'nothing', but in that 'no-thing' is an awareness of 'every-thing'. In this state there is no technique and no thoughts or feelings—just an all-pervasive quiet. Yet we are aware of everything and in full control. When we think 'this is wonderful' the quiet is broken by that thought, but we can return to the quiet simply by returning to our technique.

This is meditation.

Chapter 8

Step 4
Controlling thinking

'**W**hat if?'. How many times during the course of the disorder have we all said this in one form or another: 'what if I have an attack?','what if something happens?','what if I make a fool of myself?' How many times has the anxiety stopped us from doing what we have wanted to do? How many times have we spent days, weeks or months worrying about 'what if'? What if this is perpetuating the disorder? It is.

Thinking about it

We give our thoughts the power and our thoughts destroy our lives. Everyone is always telling us 'it is mind over matter', or 'you are always thinking about it' and 'you should just stop thinking about it'. This is exactly what we have to do. We have to stop thinking about it. We have to get to the point where it *is* mind over matter—we don't really mind because it doesn't really matter. In other words, we don't mind if we do have an attack because it doesn't really matter.

It is difficult for most people who haven't experienced a panic attack and/or anxiety to understand why we can't stop thinking about it and why we can't 'pull ourselves together'. If it were that simple we wouldn't have the disorder. It is no use trying to 'think positive', because it is extremely hard to be positive when we are living with unremitting symptoms of anxiety and ongoing attacks.

Even though we are told repeatedly that nothing is going to happen to us, it is difficult to believe when we are constantly betrayed by the attacks and anxiety. We think the next attack is going to be 'the one' in which our fears will be realized. We can't just 'not think about it' when we live and breathe it every day. This is the problem—we live and breathe it—because we constantly think it!

Changing our perception

Taking the power back means changing the way we perceive the attacks and the anxiety. We see them as being life threatening, or a threat to our sanity, or as causing us severe embarrassment. There is no doubt the anxiety can cause extreme discomfort and the attacks can feel quite violent, but they are not life threatening, nor a sign of impending insanity. We may feel as though we will be significantly embarrassed, but what is embarrassment? It is a state of mind, produced by the way we think and a point I will return to shortly. We compound the disorder by continually thinking about 'worst case scenarios'. We need to see the anxiety and the attacks for what they really are: anxiety and attacks. Nothing more.

Our thinking is so much a part of us, we don't pay any attention to the process. Without realizing it our thoughts create, dictate and control our life. All of us know the endless silent conversations, the chattering thoughts and the continual negative cycles of thinking. They roll along, carrying us with them. Yet it need not be like this. We can step in and take the power back by learning to control them. We don't have to be dictated by them. We can dictate to them. The 'what ifs' and the self absorption are part of the control we all use. Although we need to let go of them, we can also learn from them. We are creating the fear by the way we think. The 'what ifs' and the continual monitoring of our symptoms don't protect us or provide us with an 'early warning system', because they create the very symptoms we are trying to protect ourselves from.

We never take time to examine our thoughts. We don't even realize we can. We never watch the internal world of our thoughts as it spins this way and that. We react to our thoughts without realizing they are actually separate fleeting moments in time. We don't see this separateness. Instead, we believe we have no power over the continual progression of these thoughts, and the feelings caused by them. We don't see how our feelings can change within seconds of a change in our thought pattern. We can be calm one minute and anxious the next. Not seeing the progression from one thought to another and thus not seeing the progression from one feeling to another, makes it appear our anxiety and attacks are beyond our control. They aren't.

Our thoughts create the fear, which creates its own symptoms. The symptoms create the 'what ifs', which creates further symptoms. It is not so much the original stress which perpetuates the disorder, as the stress of the disorder itself. We need to be able to see how we create this stress by the fear of what we are thinking.

> We need to be in control of ourselves and our environment, yet the only thing we do not control is our thinking. We need to change this by letting go of the overall need to be in control, and control our thinking.

CASE HISTORIES

Jan

The wedding of Jan's daughter was six months away and the planning for it was gaining momentum. Instead of feeling excited, Jan was feeling desperate. What if she had a panic attack on the day of the wedding? What if she had to leave the church or the reception? What would everyone think? She didn't want to make a fool of herself or disrupt the wedding in any way. What if she couldn't even make it to the wedding at all? She was feeling anxious about it already, yet it was still six months away. Jan wanted to prevent her anxiety from increasing, but she didn't know how.

Marilyn

Marilyn's counselor had told her that clinging to the memory of her first panic attack was not helping her as she worked on her recovery. Marilyn felt quite angry with the counselor. What did the counselor know anyway? That first panic attack was dreadful. Marilyn had been in the local shopping mall when it happened. She had no idea what it was and had thought she was dying. She had asked a few people to help her, but they didn't respond. They must have thought she was either drunk or crazy. Marilyn had to get back to her car and drive herself home, where she stayed for the next four years. Although she had made it home safely every time she tried to go out since then, Marilyn would think of her first attack and naturally she would become anxious. She didn't want to go through that again. How could she not think about that attack? It was that attack which caused all the ongoing problems. Marilyn thought the counselor, like all the rest she had seen, didn't really understand and wouldn't be able to help her.

Letting go of the past

Our lack of understanding about our disorder has, in many cases, meant years of suffering, and to many people it seems that the future will be no different. One of the first things we need to do is to stop drawing on the past and projecting into the future, which incidentally is only a thought away!

It is difficult for many people to believe recovery is possible. After trying many different treatment methods without success, it is difficult to believe anything will succeed. If we think something isn't going to work, then it won't. That's our problem—our thinking.

The past belongs to the past—except for one major point. Despite the enormous difficulties we have encountered through the disorder, nothing physically has happened to us. None of our major fears have been realized, and they aren't going to be in the future. The next attack is not going to be the 'one' in which our fears come true. If anything were going to happen to us it would have happened in the first attack. We are continually drawing on our past experiences of the anxiety and attacks and projecting them into the future. We don't concentrate on what is happening now.

If we always have an attack at 7.00 a.m. we expect to have one every morning. When we have an attack we think 'I knew it would happen'. We expect to have one the following morning, and we do. We don't see what is happening now because we are too busy anticipating the next attack.

As an example, we need to be aware of our first thoughts when we wake. The first thought is usually 'where is it', and we usually feel frightened because we know 'it' is going to be there. We turn on our internal radar and check to see what is happening. We move down our body. 'I'm going to have a headache, my throat is tight, my heart is racing, I am having trouble breathing, I feel sick, I'm shaking.' And a full scale attack may develop. After it subsides we worry about the next one. As we go to sleep at night we think to ourselves, 'What if I have an attack in the morning?'

Taking back the power: awareness

The first step in learning to control our thinking is to be aware of what is actually taking place. To do this we can draw from the meditation technique, although with this exercize we will not be meditating. Part of meditation is becoming aware of when we get caught up in our thoughts. We can extend this by becoming aware of what we are thinking throughout the day and evening.

Part of us needs to stand back and observe the whole process. All we need to do at this stage is to observe our thoughts. Don't analyze them or interfere with them. Just watch them as they come tumbling in. Then bring the awareness to the body. Watch how our body responds to our thoughts and how in turn our thoughts respond to the symptoms. It isn't the symptoms which create the fear. The way we think creates the fear, which creates the symptoms, which creates further thoughts, which creates further fear and the cycle continues.

Nor do we need to be thinking about the disorder or symptoms. Whatever we are thinking about is usually negative, the mental abuse, 'I'm stupid, weak, hopeless'; the negative internal conversations; guilt; what we should have done, or shouldn't have done. The overall result is the same—anxiety and attacks. When we see this relationship, we begin to see through the fear.

> We need to become aware of the whole process of our thinking and our physical reaction to our thinking. We need to see how they build upon each other and create our symptoms.

If I ask people what they were thinking about before their last attack, they usually say that they weren't thinking of anything. This is not so. They were thinking, they just weren't aware of their thoughts. Asking the same question of people who feel continually anxious brings the same reply. They also are not aware.

We need to be aware of the relationship between our thoughts and our symptoms. When we see the relationship we will

73

understand why there is nothing to fear. The anxiety and the panic are a response to our thinking. We are simply frightening ourselves. Nothing more.

Dissociation

This technique also applies to people who dissociate first and become frightened by the altered state. 'What's happening to me. Here it comes again. I'm going insane'. We can stop the escalation into anxiety and panic simply by being aware. 'I'm dissociating.' I've just gone into a trance state'. When we acknowledge what is happening to us, without letting our thoughts race out of control, we can break the dissociated state very easily, simply by breaking our stare, by blinking our eyes a few times. When our thoughts race away with how terrible the dissociated state is, our fear will not only hold us in the altered state, but will create even more symptoms.

Taking back the power: letting go

The second stage involves letting go of our thoughts. It is not the avoidance of thoughts by trying to distract ourselves in some way, that only creates further anxiety. As in meditation, the secret of the letting-go process is not the avoidance or annihilation of our thoughts. It is the letting go of our thoughts. When we are aware of how our thoughts create our symptoms, we see we have a choice. If we keep on the rollercoaster we know where we are going to end up. Anxiety and panic.

Don't fight the thoughts. Don't try to stop the thoughts or try to avoid them. Validate the thoughts by naming them, 'anxiety' thought, 'panic' thought, 'depressive' thought, 'mental abuse' thought, 'negative' thought, 'guilt' thought and then let them go, which means we don't concentrate on them, we stop them by letting them go. This is the hard part. As soon as we let go of one thought, another is there to take its place. We let go of that and another comes.

This is where we need to have a lot of discipline. Remember, we are learning a new skill and it is going to take time and patience. In essence, what we are doing is learning to gain control over our thoughts and in doing so take back the power from the disorder. With practice, we become caught up in the letting-go process instead of becoming caught up in our thoughts.

Taking back the power: What if? So what!

When we are first learning to take the power back from our thoughts we will still have the anxiety symptoms and, in all probability, we will still experience attacks. Our normal reaction to the anxiety and the attacks is to fight them and to try and stop them from happening. This of course only increases them.

The final step in taking back the power is to feel whatever we are feeling and to let the symptoms happen without trying to control them. Of course this technique does not apply to any new symptom or sensation. Any new symptom or sensation needs to be checked out first with your doctor.

To learn to let the symptoms happen means we draw on the meditation technique again. In meditation we let go of our thoughts and we let our meditation happen without trying to control it in anyway. It is the same when we are experiencing anxiety or an attack. We do not interfere with them, we simply let the anxiety and the attack happen.

As an example, what happens when we feel happy? Do we check our body for the signs of happiness, 'my head is happy, my throat is happy, my heart beat is happy, my breathing is happy, my stomach is happy' and so on. Of course we don't. So why are we doing it with the anxiety and with the attack? We know what they are. We have an anxiety disorder. Not only have we been told our anxiety and the attacks won't hurt us physically, we are living proof they don't, so why are we constantly trying to control them? When we are happy, we feel happy and get on with whatever we are doing. If we are anxious, we can let ourself feel anxious and we can also get on with what we are doing. We don't have to get involved with it. If we have a panic attack, we let ourselves have the panic attack. If we experience the 'surge' attacks, we simply let ourselves have a 'surge' attack. We simply let them happen. We can then see it is not an attitude of 'what if', but an attitude of 'so what'.

With a 'surge' attack, when we let them happen, they disappear as quickly as they come. They can be over within thirty seconds and our racing heart and the difficulty in breathing that comes with these attacks also disappear within seconds. Letting go is the key to breaking the control we exercize over ourselves and our environment. Being able to let go, and letting the anxiety and the attacks happen, means we are finally able to take the power back. Fighting to control our anxiety and attacks perpetuates them. When we let them happen we destroy them because we are not adding to them through fear. This becomes a very powerful skill which will always be with us.

Courage

Some people will say they would never have the courage to let an attack or the anxiety happen, and that it is only natural to fight against it. I agree it is natural to want to fight against it, but fighting it by resisting it only makes it worse. We are all very strong people and we need to recognize this. Whether we use our strength and courage to take back the power by letting it happen, or whether we use it to hold onto our pervasive need to be in control, is a matter of choice. Choosing to use our strength and courage by letting the attack and the anxiety happen, will ultimately teach us why there is nothing to fear. Then we will have a choice in how we react to the attacks and anxiety in the future.

> What did you think when you read that you need to let the attack and the symptoms of anxiety happen? Did you think 'I can't do that. What will happen? How can I let it happen?' How did you respond physically? Did you feel anxious? You probably did. Most people do when they first hear this. Did the anxiety or the negative thoughts come first? It was the thoughts which came first and the symptoms which followed. Very subtle but very true.

The first time we let an attack happen there may be an increase in the intensity of the attack. This happens because we are thinking 'what if'. Go with this onrush of fear. Let this happen also. When we are able to give up the fight and give in to an attack without resisting it, it will disappear so fast it will scare us further. 'Where is it? Where did it go?' 'It' will only return if we don't let go of our fearful thinking.

When we fight the attack it can last for over an hour. When we totally give in to it and let it happen it can disappear within thirty seconds because it is not being fuelled by our fear-provoking thoughts.

What will people think?

I have often been told people can't let an attack or the anxiety happen because other people may see it happening. So what if they do. Why are we giving our mental health away to everyone else? We can spend all day trying to hide our symptoms from employers, work colleagues, family and friends. The extraordinary energy and control we use to hide our symptoms only makes us more anxious and exhausted. The more anxious we become the more we have to hide it.

Taking the power back means we cannot let the fear of what other people think get in our way of full recovery. If our hands and legs shake, let them shake. If our face turns bright red, then our face turns bright red. If we feel faint, then sit down on a chair, on the floor, on the footpath, if need be. If we vomit or have an attack of diarrhea, then we vomit or have an attack of diarrhea. Let it happen. When we let it happen, we turn off the adrenalin and it will be over as quick as it starts. We will not have to waste all of our energy trying to keep it under control and thereby turning on more adrenalin. Our mental health needs to be more important than other peoples' opinions. The feelings of embarrassment are created by our thoughts. We have to move from 'what if' to the all powerful attitude of 'so what'. 'So what' if we have an attack, 'so what' if we are feeling anxious, 'so what' if people see. So what.

Depending on how high our anxiety level is, the anxiety may not disappear as quickly. Learning to manage the anxiety by being aware of our thoughts, letting them go and by letting the anxiety be there, is part of the recovery process. As we work through the process of recovery our anxiety level diminishes, until we are anxiety-free.

- **We will reach the point where we will have a choice in how we respond, either with fear or by letting it happen. This choice will always be there. After recovery in times of extreme stress we may experience further attacks. We can choose how we respond: either with fear, 'what if', or by letting go and letting it happen. So what.**

The working through process can at times be very frustrating, but the final result is worth every step. Everything which has been taken away from us by the disorder will be given back to us through the clarity of thought and freedom which recovery brings.

Chapter 9

Step 5
Working through to recovery

The working-through process

Recovery is not as simple as we would like it to be. In the beginning, it feels as though we take one step forward then two steps backwards. This is why so many people feel they are never going to recover. It is also part of the reason why so many people become discouraged and give up.

We need to understand the step-by-step process of working through the various stages of recovery. Understanding the working-through process is of the utmost importance, yet it is rarely discussed as an issue.

Patience

One of the first things we need to learn is patience. Everyone, naturally enough, wants recovery now. Not tonight, not tomorrow, not next week, but this very second. This creates further stress which keeps the whole cycle going. Whether we like it or not, we all have to learn patience, with the working-through process and with ourselves. Learning to be patient with ourselves is learning to be kind to ourselves. Being kind to ourselves means we are not putting ourselves under any further unnecessary stress.

We need to direct our energy into the determination to commit ourselves, time and again, to the working-through process despite setbacks.

Our threshold to stress

The working-through process may at first seem difficult and confusing, but it isn't. Some people can feel daunted and overwhelmed by the amount of effort needed. It is worth it. Everything which is required from us during the working-through process will be given back to us in the sheer joy and total freedom of recovery.

The working-through process is the same for everyone. The only difference is our personal threshold to stress. Some people may have reached the point where they cannot tolerate even the smallest stress. Other people may have a higher threshold to stress, but it is still low enough to trigger fearful thoughts.

The time it takes people to recover will vary. The individual threshold to stress comes into account, but the amount of effort and discipline we put into our recovery is most important.

The first attack was the result of either a build-up of stress or a major life stress. In other words, the anxiety and/or attack happened when we reached the limit of our individual threshold to stress. This doesn't mean we are weak. It simply means we have reached our limit to stress, just as most people will reach their limit to stress at one point or other in their life. Continual worry about the symptoms of anxiety and attacks only increases our stress and lowers our threshold to it.

As we begin the working-through process it is helpful if we have an understanding of how low our threshold to stress is and how high our anxiety is. Using the scale (Figure 9.1) will help us to estimate our levels.

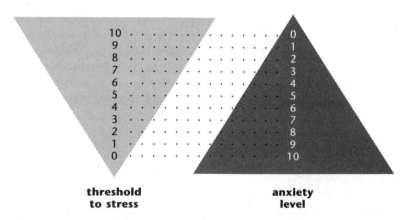

threshold
to stress

anxiety
level

Figure 9.1

If our threshold to stress is now extremely low we may not be able to tolerate even the smallest daily stress. Our threshold to stress would be zero, while our anxiety level would be ten. At level five we would be able to tolerate the daily stress/es, but would find our anxiety level rising if there is a break in our normal daily routine. At level ten we would be able to deal with almost any stress without becoming anxious.

The working-through process means working to increase our threshold to stress back to normal levels, while decreasing our anxiety level.

> It's no use just hearing or reading about panic anxiety management skills. We have to practice them. There have been occasions when we say we're not getting any better, and nothing has changed. If we are not getting results it usually means we are not practicing enough, or even not practicing at all!

Back to basics

Understanding setbacks

Setbacks are unavoidable. In fact, the more we have the better! Each setback teaches us more about ourselves and our disorder, and strengthens and refines our management skills. To work through to recovery we need to understand why setbacks happen.

As an example, our threshold to stress may now be at level zero. Practicing our management skills will raise our threshold to stress to level one. We then experience our first breakthrough—we feel no fear or anxiety. This brings a complete clarity of thought and a total sense of freedom. Any stress higher than level one will be enough to start the whole vicious cycle again. Inevitably, this happens and we have a setback.

It is not so much the stress itself which causes the setback as how we think about it. When a stress is higher than our threshold, we automatically slip back into our old way of thinking. Anxiety and attacks follow. We become so caught up in it that we are not even aware that we have fallen back into the cycle. Only when we become aware of it can we do something about it.

Identifying the stress will show why the setback has happened. Whatever the stress is, it will be higher than we can tolerate at this point. If we are working from zero, identification is not difficult, as the normal day-to-day stress will trigger the automatic cycle of thinking.

When we become aware of why it has happened, the next step is to resolve any issues relating to the stress and to let the setback happen. Our threshold to stress will continue to rise as long as we continue with management skills. We will then reach level two. Any stress higher than level two will trigger a set back. Again we go through the principles outlined above. This is when we need to have patience. This is the working-through process.

Steps in the working-through process:

- Isolate the stress/es
- Be aware of how we are thinking about them
- Resolve any issues relating to the stress
- Let go of anxiety-producing thoughts
- Let the setback happen
- Continue with meditation
- Continue to work with our thinking

If we are working from level zero, the first breakthrough usually only lasts for about an hour as the daily stress will trigger the automatic way of thinking. With continued practice of the above, our threshold to stress will continue to rise. We will begin to experience days and then weeks of clarity and freedom. When we have a setback after these periods, everything does seem much worse and more hopeless. It isn't. Only the comparison between these two ways of being makes it appear so. We will reach the point where there are no more setbacks. Clarity of thought and the sense of freedom will then become our automatic way of thinking and feeling.

If we are not sure why we are having a setback, we can write a list of everything that is currently happening in our life. There may be family problems, a difficult financial or work situation, children home on school holidays. There can be many reasons.

CASE HISTORIES

Betty

Betty had worked extremely hard on her recovery. She had been able to return to work three months ago and was really happy to be back in the workforce. Although she'd had the occasional bad day, Betty was able to work through them and she had begun to feel that she had finally recovered. That was until last week. Now Betty was beginning to think the disorder was returning. Her anxiety was increasing and the attacks had returned. She knew that returning to work had been stressful, but she was happy in her job. She couldn't understand why the anxiety and the attacks were back. To all intents and purposes life was normal. Her husband and children were fine. Although Betty realized it was hard to run a household and work at the same time, she felt it was worth the extra effort. Her father's death two months ago had been traumatic but she felt that couldn't be the reason. Betty wondered if it was the argument she had had with her mother and sisters. The issues had still not been resolved and each time they were together the atmosphere was quite tense. She knew the anxiety and the attacks were making her feel tense, but she couldn't understand why they had come back. Betty thought that she needed to be more aware of what was causing stress in her life!

David

David had been making little progress with his recovery and was becoming disillusioned with the recovery program. He was having difficulty in finding any time to himself to concentrate on his recovery. There were so many other things which needed to be done first. He had volunteered to take on extra duties at work because of staff shortages. That meant he wasn't getting home until 7.00 p.m. Working late meant he spent less time with his children, so he did his best to make up for it on weekends. This interfered with the work he did for two service clubs in his area, but he tried to juggle his time. This in turn was complicated by the fact that his neighbours and friends were always dropping by with various requests for favors or help. On top of all this he had to stop and take time out when the anxiety and the attacks became too much. Having to find time to work on his recovery was the final straw. David was feeling quite resentful because he thought there should be some sort of recovery program which took all these demands on his time into account.

To complete our list, write down how many times we have taken time out to meditate or practice some other form of relaxation. Then estimate how much time we have put into working with our thinking. That usually gives us the complete answer.

Illness can also lower our threshold. Many people react to the additional symptoms with further anxiety and panic. We need to realize that if we are unwell, we would have these new symptoms even if we did not have the disorder. Don't add to them. Let go of the anxiety-producing thoughts.

Remember, we mustn't spend time and energy continually worrying about the setback and thinking we'll never get over the disorder. We will with practice and patience.

Making decisions

There are certain situations where we may be under stress, but feel we cannot do anything about them. We can spend days and nights worrying. As hard as the situation may be, we need to understand how it is affecting us. If we have done everything we can do and the situation remains unchanged, we need to let go of the worry. Sometimes these situations may revolve around other family members or friends and may be extremely serious. It comes back to making a decision to let go of the worry. We are only losing valuable energy worrying or trying to change a situation we can't.

Sometimes there are very difficult decisions to be made. Once we make a decision we need to let it rest. Many people use their energy continually reviewing the decision. It doesn't matter whether our decision is ultimately right or wrong. Worrying about a decision is putting our recovery on hold. Our recovery must be our number one priority.

Recovery: our number one priority

This is a very important point. Many people do not give their recovery priority. Although everyone wants to recover, there can seem a million more important things to be done first. Our recovery has to become the most important thing in our life.

Our loyalty has to be to ourselves. This can be very difficult for many of us because we feel we are being selfish in putting our own needs first. How can working towards our recovery be selfish? In the working-through process, especially at the beginning, we need all of our energies for ourselves.

The lack of understanding by those close to us can create extra stress. All of us are extremely sensitive and vulnerable to other people's suggestions or ideas, even if it means doing the opposite to what we feel is right for us. Part of the recovery process means accepting that we don't have to go along with what other people expect from us. We don't have to do, or accept, anything we know is going to be detrimental to ourselves and/or our recovery. Like everyone else, we have the right to do what is right for us.

Cognitive behavioral exposure program

A cognitive behavioral therapist will normally work with various types of exposure methods pertaining to our particular anxiety disorder. When we begin to work with our avoidance behavior we will probably feel anxious and the 'what ifs' may return. In only a few seconds the 'what ifs' can create a mountain of fear and anxiety which seems insurmountable. We may forget any management strategies we have learnt, and become caught up in the automatic cycle of thinking.

It is most important to realize that we will feel anxious and frightened when working with a CBT program. By accepting this we can work with it, not against it.

Making allowances

As an example, part of our CBT program may include doing the shopping alone. This can be broken down into easy steps. To begin with, we can go to the shop early in the morning. We will feel more comfortable in letting the anxiety and attack happen if the shop is not too crowded. As we become more confident in letting it happen, we can begin to shop at different times of the day.

If part of our program means going to dinner or the theatre, we can ask to be seated by an aisle or an exit, or both–not so much for a quick getaway, but to help break down the feeling of being trapped. The aisle or exit is there if we do need to leave quickly. If we work with our thinking and let the anxiety and attack happen, we will find we won't have to leave.

Making allowances is not giving in; it is working with the disorder. Doing nothing is giving in. In the early stages of recovery, making allowances helps us to reduce the amount

85

of pressure we feel. Making allowances indefinitely means
we are not putting ourselves under enough pressure!

Another example of an allowance is breaking down the time we know we will have to spend in any given situation. It may be a business meeting, it may be an evening with friends, it may be doing the shopping. It could be anything.

If we know something will take two hours, work with the first hour first. Don't even think about the second hour. If it is too difficult and our anxiety level doesn't settle down, we can leave after the first hour. Usually by the second hour we are not even aware the first hour is over, because we have become involved with what we are doing, and not with the anxiety and attacks.

In the beginning there may be times when we feel we will have to leave a situation. If it becomes too difficult to manage, then leave, not with a sense of failure, but accepting that this time it was too difficult. A sense of failure defeats us, not only in the short term but also in the long term. Accept it and let go of the worrying. There will be other times when we will be able to do it as long as we keep practicing.

We become ultra-sensitive to ourselves, and tend to think other people's reactions towards us are as intensified as our own. In fact, a situation which we consider devastating is either unnoticed by other people or is quickly forgotten by them. Don't add unnecessary stress by worrying about what people have thought or will think. It is not important. Recovery is.

The question sometimes arises about how much we need to practise a CBT program in order to reduce our avoidance behavior. Having to confront various situations and places we have avoided does initially place us under more stress. We need to learn to walk a fine line. There are going to be times when we feel we want to give up and we begin to despair of ever recovering. There may be times when we feel this way, but we continually push ourselves without being aware of how much more anxiety is being generated. Then we do give up through exhaustion and despair.

Working with our avoidance behavior, and the whole process of recovery, means we need to learn to care of ourselves. We need to learn when it is appropriate to pull back and take a break, as long as the break doesn't go on for weeks. After the break, begin again.

Begin again. These two words can mean so much in the working-through process. If we feel that we are not making progress, if we feel that some of our attempts didn't quite work out the way we would have liked, let them go and *begin again.*

> Our ultra-sensitivity also increases the sense of guilt we feel towards our families because we can't do everything we would like to do. We need to be aware of the extra stress caused by this. We can spend a week worrying and feeling guilty over one small incident which we think of as a failure. Guilt only increases our anxiety. It keep us locked into the cycle. We need to let it go, so we can move forward to recovery and to the time when we will be able to do everything we haven't been able to do.

Acceptance

Our levels of acceptance fluctuates during the working-through process. When we have a setback we get caught up in our old ways of thinking and feeling. Some people may again start to doubt they have the disorder, and begin to worry that the diagnosis may be incorrect.

Non-acceptance means we are only making the situation worse for ourselves. We all have periods of doubt about the diagnosis. If this does happen it is important to go back and talk with our doctor.

Compounding this doubt are the anxiety symptoms and how they change. Once we get on top of one symptom, another one takes its place. Any new symptom needs to be checked by our doctor, and sometimes we may feel like a hypochondriac. However, it is more important for us to know what the new symptoms are, instead of continually worrying. If we are told the new symptom is another anxiety symptom, we need to accept the diagnosis and not get caught in the vicious circle again.

Motivation

Another important point is our motivation. If it has dropped, we need to look at why. A drop in motivation also means a drop in the will to take power. Sometimes our lack of motivation can be caused by fears of change and of growth.

The working-through process means we are getting in touch with ourselves, perhaps for the first time. We become aware of how we think and react on a day-to-day basis, which usually gives us insights into ourselves which we have not had before.

Sometimes these insights can be quite threatening, as they could signal the need for changes in our life.

The drop in motivation may mean we are avoiding these insights. Everyone wants to recover, but many of us want recovery to mean we will return to our former self. The working-through process means we are getting in touch with ourselves, with feelings, needs and desires we may never have known existed. These will need to be integrated and their integration will mean not a return to the old, but the birth of the new.

Have a look and see if fear of change has caused the drop in motivation. Become aware of how those fears are holding you back.

Psychotherapy

At this stage of the process some people may go into psychotherapy. As was discussed in chapter four, psychotherapy can be extremely beneficial. Many of us who have an anxiety disorder have suppressed our primary emotions of anger, grief and so on. Psychotherapy helps us contact these feelings. Experiencing them is part of the healing process.

People have asked the question of what to do with their thoughts while working through issues in psychotherapy. There will be issues in therapy which need to be thought through and worked with, and they may cause anxiety and attacks. Again, it means walking a fine line. Be aware of why they have occurred and let them happen.

As our management skills increase we will begin to realize a subtle pattern emerging with our anxiety and attacks. When we are avoiding confronting particular personal issues, or in other words, not being honest with ourselves, we may find ourselves reacting with anxiety or an attack. We can use these subtle guides to get to know and understand ourselves on a deeper level.

Taking care of ourselves

A proper diet and enough sleep are also very important in helping raise our threshold to stress. If we have eating problems it is important we seek advice to help re-establish normal eating patterns.

Returning to healthier sleep patterns can be difficult, and this is where the meditation technique can play an important role.

Although we have developed our daily meditation routine, our meditation technique can also be used at night to help us go to sleep. In this case, instead of going into meditation we can let the meditation technique take us gently and easily into sleep.

Exercise also plays an important part in the recovery process, and it would be helpful to seek advice in establishing a regular exercise program.

Relearning

The working-through process also involves relearning what it is like to be 'normal'. We lose sight of what it is like to be 'normal', and it is not unusual for people to interpret 'normalcy' as a setback! It isn't, we just have to relearn.

This means relearning to have a 'normal' bad day without reacting with fear that 'it is all coming back'. Returning to 'normal' means we will have bad days, just like everyone else.

We will probably have days when we feel unwell. It doesn't mean a return of the disorder—it means we are feeling unwell. We need to make sure we are eating properly and getting enough sleep. If not, we will feel tired and irritable just like everyone does when they neglect themselves.

Recovery is worth every step. At times the working-through process is difficult. Don't lose sight of the overall picture which can be changed from one of fear and anxiety to one of clarity and freedom.

Chapter 10

In search of self

Who am I?

Panic anxiety management skills allow many of us to be free of our anxiety disorder. The skills can give us a control over our lives that we have never had before; but sometimes even this isn't enough. A little-known aspect of the working-through process can hold us back, and be the final factor in the perpetuation of the disorder. It is our lack of sense of self.

Although this aspect is not related only to anxiety disorders, it can be the single most important issue in the disorders. Despite our ongoing attacks and anxiety, it can be the one issue we are most concerned about. It is as if we intuitively know the root cause of our suffering.

The lack of identification goes beyond our cry of 'this is not me'. When we say 'this is not me' we are referring to the image we had before the disorder. Despite the image we had of ourselves, we have always known that we never felt any sense of who we are. We never had a real sense of self. This essential element was always lacking in our lives, and it is from this that our feelings of inadequacy, lack of confidence and lack of self-esteem arose.

We counteracted these by our need to be perfect. Over the years we adapted and modified our behavior to what we perceived were other people's expectations of us. We became who we thought we should be, and in doing so suppressed much of who we could be. Our identity became dependent on other people's perceptions of us. The more dependent we became, the more we had to suppress our real self, even if we didn't realize we were doing it. The more we suppressed our self, the more inadequate we felt. The more inadequate we felt, the more we felt the need to be perfect.

Over the years we built the image of who we thought we should be. We lived our lives with an uneasy feeling that we were not who we appeared to be. If we were not who we appeared to be, then who were we? We didn't know. We were never able to answer the question.

The anxiety and/or the attacks blasted into our lives. They pushed past our control and steamrolled our defenses. The image we had of ourselves crumbled with the weight of its own illusion. The disintegration of ourselves continued and our seemingly solid foundations of our self and our life were torn down.

Suddenly we were thrown back onto ourselves and we had nothing left as an identity. Our sense of inadequacy, our lack of confidence and lack of self-esteem became predominant. We felt helpless and isolated. Our need to be in control was the only defense we had left. We tightened our grip on it because we felt that total annihilation of ourselves was only an attack away.

We became separated from our real selves through a lifetime of suppression and, when we needed it most, we felt that we had nothing to give us strength or support. Our sense of helplessness and isolation increased dramatically. These feelings of helplessness and isolation are a measure of the degree to which we are separate from our self. It is the ultimate separation anxiety.

All of us search for external answers to our difficulties, but we don't realize we are looking in the wrong direction. Although we may find temporary measures to sustain us, we don't recognize or feel the enormous potential of our self which is waiting to assist us.

Destruction to construction

The seemingly inherent negativity of the disorder can actually be the most positive experience of our life. How many other people are given such an opportunity! The disorder has done so much of the hard work for us. It has stripped away the image of who we thought we should be, and has returned us to the basis of who we could be.

Life isn't just about growing up, having a career, getting married, having children and so on. These are things we *do* during life, but they are not life. Life is continual evolution and development.

Our need to be in control of ourselves and our environment is our unconscious effort to try to stop this change. Although there are many external changes in our life, we fight to control any internal changes and development of ourselves. We need to be in control to keep the image we have, and the image other people have, of ourselves. We haven't been able to let our image change in case it meant we did not meet the expectations of other people. We are now paying dearly for this.

Our continual suppression of self means we have blocked the ongoing development of our self. Although we have always wanted to be able to express and develop our self, we have never been willing to take the risk. How many times have we ignored the call to self, or not heard its almost silent whisperings? This time it is not whispering. It is shouting.

> Anxiety disorders are destructive. They tear away the very fabric of our whole being. They destroy our way of life. The attacks and the anxiety terrify us sometimes to the extent that normal everyday living is non-existent. Yet we do not recognize in this destruction an equally positive force. The destruction can be a positive turning point in becoming our real self.

Insight

As we begin to practice awareness, we become aware of our own behavior and our subtle motivations. Slowly and subtly these insights into our self break through. What was initially destruction can become construction.

When the insights first come they are fleeting glimpses of how we could be. They disappear and reappear as we begin to assimilate them and begin to build on them. We begin to see that responsibility for our peace and happiness is ours, and ours alone. We cannot shift the responsibility of ourselves to other people or to other factors.

Sometimes we are able to assimilate the insights easily, at other times it calls for hard work. Sometimes the insights can herald changes so basic they are accompanied by fear.

As we become aware of these insights we begin to see we are letting go of more than the disorder. Life begins to take on a different meaning. Our ideals and values change. Things which were once important to us no longer seem so, yet it appears there is nothing else to take their place.

This can be very threatening and disturbing, despite our desperate longings to be ourselves. The pre-disorder identity has gone; its place was taken by the 'disordered' identity. This in turn is breaking down, leaving us no sense of identity, no sense of self, to take its place. The feeling of total annihilation can seem closer than ever before.

The fear of change

We need to stop and realize that there have been other times in our life when we have made major changes. Although these changes were external, we still feared change because we did not really know what lay ahead. We may have felt this fear when we started work, went to university, got married or had children. That fear is the same as we are feeling now. If we can remember those other occasions we will see this fear is not unique. We have felt it before. Back then, we went ahead and did what we had to do, still feeling unsure, still feeling the fear, the aloneness and isolation. This time, although the changes are internal, the fear is no different.

All we know at this stage is that we are walking into unknown territory and it can seem easier to stop where we are, despite our unresolved difficulties. What we don't know is that the unknown territory is that of the self. As the 'disordered' self breaks down it can mean the birth of our real self.

The birth of the new

It is unknown and unfamiliar. The dawning sense of self is like living with a person we don't know, living with a person whose values and needs are different. Having to welcome such a stranger into our life on such an intimate level is naturally frightening, even though the stranger is ourself.

This is one of the most confusing aspects of the working-through process. As we learn to face the attacks, the anxiety and the fear we may also have to learn to face the fear of change and the fear of the new emerging self. The carefully constructed defenses of a lifetime have been torn down. Rebuilding on more solid foundations means we have to push past the new fears.

When the new fears emerge we will have already broken through many barriers and overcome many of the fears associated with the disorder. We will be able to push past these new fears also, but it must be done gently and intuitively.

The essence of who we are, the essence of our self, is intact. It has always been there and will always be there. Now we have a chance to get to know our self. Now we have the chance to develop and integrate it into our life.

The process is hard, but each step we take means we learn more about the process. In the beginning it is difficult; there is fear, there is anger, there is frustration. 'Why do I have to go through this, why can't I just be normal like everyone else?' What is 'normal' anyway? Use the anger, the fear and frustration to push past these new fears. With each step we gain new awareness, new knowledge and increased strength. The process becomes easier and more tolerable. This is life, this is growth, a continual evolution. Now we can work with it by letting go and flowing with it, not by trying to control it.

A time of learning

At times we will feel tired, defenseless and vulnerable. These feelings don't last. We will begin to know and understand why we are feeling this way. We will get to know quite a lot about our self, in fact, sometimes we will wish we didn't know so much! It is a time of learning to listen to the inner voice of the self, which is more than willing to help us. If we stop and take the time to listen, the inner voice will be our guide. All too often we do not hear ourselves.

At some points it may mean rearranging things to make life a little more comfortable and a little bit easier while the integration with the self is worked through. Again, it is a time of learning what our needs are, perhaps learning new skills or trying things we have always wanted to do. Rejecting some, embracing others we didn't know were there.

We have to become aware we do have a choice in everything. In making the choice we need to be aware of its implications. We can choose and set limits if we need to. We can choose to move at our own pace. It is going to feel unfamiliar, we will feel vulnerable and the fear will be there, but so too is the self's determination to grow.

We must learn to trust our self. Getting to know our self helps us gain that trust. It is taking risks with our self.

CASE HISTORIES

Jane

It was one of those beautiful autumn evenings. The light from the setting sun filtered through the trees and their leaves blazed with colour. Jane wondered how many other people were looking at this natural masterpiece as they hurried home after the day's work. Jane knew that she had never taken much notice before. Now was different. Once or twice a day she would be struck by the beauty of her surroundings. A moment here, a moment there. But those moments were precious in their spontaneity. They added to the peace she felt within herself. She was amazed at the last few years of her life. It had not always been like this. The years of panic disorder/agoraphobia had appeared to take everything from her. They were desolate years. The fight back was long and hard but she knew now it had been worth it. Everything that had been taken away from her had been given back a thousand-fold. She was at peace with herself and she was free.

Peter

Peter was exhilarated. It was early morning and he had reached halfway in a 10 km bike ride along the coast road. He wished he had brought his camera. Peter had loved photography ever since he was a child. He had always wanted to be a photographer, and now he was one. He thought of his parents. They had both worked long and hard to pay for his university fees, and they were proud of him when he received his PhD and entered the world of academia. Panic disorder/agoraphobia had changed all that. As Peter progressed towards recovery he realized that academic life was not for him. He struggled silently with the realization for three years because he didn't want to let his parents down. He even studied for another degree, hoping to combat his disquiet. It didn't work, and he made the break to follow his dream of being a photographer. He knew he was taking a risk, but he also knew it was worth it. He was free.

In letting ourselves take risks we will develop more confidence in our own ability. It doesn't matter if we make mistakes along the way. Mistakes are a part of living. Mistakes are actually our teachers if we are willing to learn from them. If we don't learn from them, we repeat them in one form or another.

At each step we can take what we need and let go of what we must. The development of the self is like the birth of a child. We need to be protective of it. The conscious feel of it will be so new, it will feel vulnerable.

People around us will not be able to understand our inner pressure. We are meeting the push for growth head-on, and at this stage we are doing it for our self. This is all that matters at this point. The question of selfishness may come up again. Is being free from the disorder selfish? Is wanting to develop our full potential selfish? Look what happened last time we didn't!

This may be a time when counselling can help ourselves and our families get to know and accept the person we are becoming.

> **The ultimate answer and the ultimate resources are within us. It can sometimes hurt and it can sometimes be frightening. It can mean different things for all of us, but ultimately it is the path to freedom. It is the path of self determination.**

The path to freedom

Being afraid is all right. Being hesitant is all right. Feeling vulnerable and defenseless is all right. They are all part of the ongoing development of our self. When we begin to work with it, we won't know where we are, where we are going and what will happen to us along the way. This is all right too.

There is no exact blueprint on how to get to know our self, no external guide or map we can look at. The blueprint is our self. How to read the map means reading our self. The guide is our self and it will show us how to work through the various stages. From the first step to the last, it will be an individual journey. But what a journey!

As we let the process continue we begin to trust our self and we begin to trust the process. We begin to see familiar landmarks and we begin to see the bridges we need to cross. We get to know the rest stops on the way and we know with growing certainty that we are headed in the right direction.

It does mean changes, but all the resources necessary will be found in our self and we will find them waiting for us at each step. Not only will we find them waiting, we will find they have been there all along. There will be times of uncertainty when we turn back or stop along the way. When we are ready to begin again, we will find the resources are still there.

What does fear hold us back from? Being free. Self-expression. What do we want for ourselves in five years time? Who do we want to be? That person is not going to magically appear one morning. We must work towards being that person. It is a journey in ourselves to ourselves.

All the energy which has been used to suppress our self, can be freed for us to use in whatever way we wish. It is a gift of life which is waiting for all of us. The time will come again for change, far less dramatically, but come again it will and there will be new challenges to meet. This call for growth is part of the evolutionary development in all of us. It is a question of how honest we are being with ourselves, but this honesty is the way of self determination. Of individuation.

It is our choice.

Chapter 11

Questions and answers

Question

A friend of mine has told me alternative therapies such as massage or acupuncture will help me. I'm not sure if I should try them.

Answer

Massage and acupuncture can help to release and balance bodily tensions. As with all other therapies, we need to learn to control and manage the anxiety and attacks ourselves. While we are learning the management skills, massage and acupuncture can be useful in reducing anxiety and tension. In the long term they can help keep our bodies relaxed.

Question

I am not happy about taking prescribed medications and I am wondering if herbal medications and vitamin therapy would help me instead.

Answer

Herbal and vitamin preparations are used regularly by many people. They can be bought over the counter or prescribed by an herbalist or naturopath. They can be helpful in easing the condition, but again they do not teach us the necessary skills for the long-term management of the disorder.

There is, however, one note of caution regarding these and other medications. Some people have reactions to them which are put down to anxiety; yet when the medication is discontinued the reactions disappear. If we are using these preparations, we must be aware of how we feel after taking them. We should not assume any new sensation or symptom is part of the disorder. It may be a reaction to the medication.

Question

I am not sure what is meant by 'letting the anxiety and the attacks happen'. They are so much a part of my life I don't know how to separate them from myself.

Answer

When we are feeling happy, we don't continually monitor our feeling of happiness or think of how happy we are, we just let the feeling of happiness be there as we get on with whatever we are doing. The same applies to the feelings of anxiety and the attacks. We can separate ourselves from them simply by noting them, 'this is anxiety, this is an attack'. We just let them be there, without concentrating on them. Not concentrating on them allows us to concentrate on other aspects of our lives. The same is true for temporary feelings of depression. We need to be aware of why we are depressed and we let ourselves be depressed, but we don't become the depression. If we don't add to it by continually worrying about how depressed we are, it will disappear because we are not fueling it. Of course, it does depend on the degree of your depression. If the depression stays with you it will need to be treated by your therapist.

Question

Will hypnosis help?

Answer

Hypnotism can produce a very positive response in the short term. The result will not last if we have no understanding of the disorder and don't know how to manage the attacks and anxiety ourselves. In conjunction with panic/anxiety management skills, hypnotism can help while we work with aspects of the disorder. If we use an audio tape of the hypnosis session during periods of high anxiety and attacks, the tape must teach us how to control the anxiety and the attacks. The control does not come from a cassette tape.

Some people use subliminal tapes in an effort to ease their symptoms. We must know what the subliminal message of the tape is and, more importantly, we should consciously know and learn how to manage anxiety and the attacks ourselves.

Question

I have heard about people becoming housebound. I am the opposite. I can't bear to be in the house. As soon as my husband goes to work I have to get out of the house. I spend my days travelling on buses or walking around shopping centres. Is this part of the disorder?

Answer

This does happen to some people. If they have difficulty in being alone, going out and being around other people is better than staying home. It can also happen to people who were housebound, but for another reason. As people progress in their recovery, some may go through a stage where the thought of being home all day brings back too many memories of their disorder. They prefer to go out as much as they can. This stage does pass.

Question

If I recover, how can I be sure the disorder won't come back?

Answer

Using the management skills and working through the process of recovery will teach you about yourself and the disorder. You will always have the skills and the knowledge you have gained, and they will help prevent a return of the disorder. By the way, what do you mean by 'if'?

Bibliography

American Psychiatric Association 1980, *Diagnostic and Statistical Manual of Mental Disorders*, 3rd edn, APA, Washington.

American Psychiatric Association 1994, *Diagnostic and Statistical Manual of Mental Disorders*, 4th edn, APA, Washinton.

Andrews G., Peters L., Teesson M., 1994, 'The Measurement of Consumer Outcomes in Mental Health', *Australian Health Ministers Advisory Council*, Australian Govt Publishing Service.

Argyle, N. & Roth, 1990, 'The phenomenological study of 90 patients with panic disorder', Psychiatric Developments, 7, pp.187–209, cited in 'The structure of Phobias in Panic Disorder', N. Argyle, C. Solyom, and L. Solyom, 1991, *British Journal of Psychiatry*, 159, pp.378–82.

Arthur-Jones, J, and Fox, B, 1994, 'Cross Cultural Comparisons of Panic Disorder' Centre for Stress and Anxiety Management, Eastwood SA.

Australian Bureau of Statistics, 1995, 'Estimated Resident Population by Sex and Age for States and Territory of Asutralia: June 1994 and preliminary June 1995', ABS Catalgue no 3201.0.

Benson, H. 1975, *The Relaxation Response*, William Morrow, New York.

Boyd, J.H. & Crump, T. 1991, 'Westphal's Agoraphobia', *Journal of Anxiety Disorders* 5, pp. 77–86.

Brown G.W. & Harris T.O., 1993, 'Aetiology of anxiety and depressive disorders in an inner-city population. 1. Early adversity', *Psychological Medicine*, 23, 143–54.

Brayley, J., Bradshaw, G. & Pols, R. 1991, *Guidelines for the Prevention and Management of Benzodiazepine Dependence*, AGPS, Canberra.

Brunton P 1965, 'The Quest of the Overself', Samuel Weiser Inc., York Beach, Maine.

Commission of Public Affairs and the Division of Public Affairs of the American Psychiatrists Association 1990, *Information Booklet on Anxiety Disorders*, APA, Washington.

Cox, B.J., Norton, G.R., Swinson, R.P. & Endler, N.S. 1990, 'Substance abuse and panic related anxiety, a critical review', *Behav. Res. Therapy* 28, 5, pp. 385–93.

Evans, L. 1995, 'A Follow-up of an Agoraphobia Treatment Program', Commonwealth Dept of Human Services and Health.

Fewtrell, W.D. & O'Connor, K.P. 1988, 'Dizziness and Depersonalisation', *Adv. Behav. Res. Ther.*, vol 10, pp.201–18

Kabat-Zinn, J., Massion, A.,Kristeller, J., Peterson, L.G.,Fletcher, K.E., Pbert, L., Lenderking and Santorelli S.F. 1992 'Effectiveness of a Meditation-Based Stress Reduction Program in the Treatment of Anxiety Disorders', *American Journal of Psychiatry*, vol.149, no.7, pp.936–43.

Kenardy J., Oei T.P.S., Ryan P, Evans L, 1988, 'Attribution of Panic Attacks: Patient Perspective', *Journal of Anxiety Disorders*, vol.2, pp.243–51.

Malison, R.T. & Price, L.H. 1990, 'Panic states', *Current Opinions In Psychiatry* 3, pp.229–34.

Oswald I, 1962, *Sleeping and Waking: Physiology and Psychology*, Elsevier Publishing Company, Amsterdam.

Otto, M.W., Gould, R.A., Pollack, M.H. 1994, 'Cognitive-Behavioural Treatment of Panic Disorder: Considerations for the Treatment of Patients Over the Long Term', *Psychiatric Annals*, vol.24, no.6.

Phobic Trust of New Zealand 1991, *Phobos*, vol.5, no.7.

Putman, F.W., 1989, 'Diagnosis and Treatment of Multiple Personality Disorder', Guildford Press, New York.

Sheehan, D., Ballenger, J. & Jacobsen, G. 1980, 'Treatment of endogenous anxiety with phobic, hysterical and hypochondrical symptoms', *Archives of General Psychiatry* 37, pp. 51–9, cited in 'Economic & life consequences experienced by a group of individuals with panic disorder', L. Siegel, W. Jones, & J. Wilson, 1990, *Journal of Anxiety Disorders* 4, pp.201–11.

Tart C.T., 1972, *Altered States of Consciousness*, Doubleday Anchor, New York.

Task Force on Meditation, 1977, 'Position statement on meditation', *American Journal of Psychiatry* 134, 720, cited in Kutz et al. 1985, 'Dynamic psychotherapy, the relaxation response and mindfulness meditation', *American Journal of Psychiatry*, 142, pp.1–7.

Uhde T.W., 1994, *Principles and Practice of Sleep Medicine,* 2nd edn, ch. 84, W.B.Saunders & Co.

Weekes, C. 1992, *Self Help For Your Nerves*, 28th edn, Angus & Robertson, Sydney.

Further information

For further information and the names of therapists or organizations in your state you may contact the following organizations by phone or through their websites. Please carefully interview any therapist you call for help with this disorder, regarding their experience and methods. This list is for your information only and does not constitute a personal reference for any individual clinician, but should bring you the names of people who are experienced with the cognitive-behavioral methods of treating anxiety disorders. There are hundreds of agencies and pages of information listed on the WWW.

General Information and Referral Lists
Panic Anxiety Education Management Service
P.O. Box 258
Fullarton, So. Australia 5063
Phone: 61 88339 4998
Website: http://www.paems.com.au/index.html
This is the service in Australia co-directed by author Bronwyn Fox and Jasmine Arthur-Jones. Their website includes extensive information about anxiety disorders and panic attacks, international referral information (including the U.S.), research data, a question and answer section, and a 24-hour chat line.

Anxiety Disorder Association of America
11900 Parklawn Dr., Ste. 100
Rockville MD 20852
Website: http://www.adad.org/5_con/5e_01.htm
This organization and website has a list of therapists who specialize in anxiety disorders, including their credentials. It also has information about self-help groups, annual conferences, and membership.

National Institute of Mental Health
5600 Fishers Lane, Room 7C-02, MSC 8030
Bethesda, MD 20892-8030
Website: http.//www.nimh.nih.gov/anxiety/index.htm
Phone 1-68-88-ANXIETY
Lists specific detailed information about anxiety disorders and panic attacks, including many resources i.e. books, videos, free pamphlets, information on referrals, medications, research, and news.

A few clinics and agencies that specialize in anxiety disorders:
Andover Center
166 No. Main St.
Andover MA 01810
Phone 978 475-7249
Dr. Jorge DeNamali M.D. Medical Director

The Anxiety Clinic
4843 E. Thomas Rd. Ste.6
Phoenix, AZ 85018-7740
Thomas Richards, Ph.D.

Open Doors Institute of California
13601 Ventura Blvd., Ste. 600
Sherman Oaks, CA 91423
818-710-6442
Lynne Freeman, Ph.D.
Website: http.//opendoorsinstitute.com
Individual on-site therapy, and phone therapy.

The Pendulum Organization
8221 Brecksville Rd. Bldg. 4#104
Brecksville OH 44141
Transitions Program
Gene Benedetto Ph.D., Director
http.//onestepatatime.com
Active website program with over 700 members who participate in a
discussion forum, chat room, pen pals and on-line support groups.

Self-help groups:
Agoraphobics in Motion (A.I.M.)
1719 Crooks Royal Oak MI. 48067-1306
248 547-0400
13 national groups that use specific behavioral and cognitive techniques
to help people with agoraphobia, anxiety and panic attacks.

Agoraphobics Building Independent Lives (ABIL)
3805 Cutshaw Ave. Ste. 450
Richmond, VA 23230
804 353 3964
28 national self-help groups

INDEX